# stitch | craft create QUICK KNITS

OVER 25 APPEALING PROJECTS THAT ARE QUICK AND SIMPLE TO KNIT

# *stitch | craft*
# create QUICK KNITS

D&C

David and Charles

www.stitchcraftcreate.co.uk/ideas

# Contents

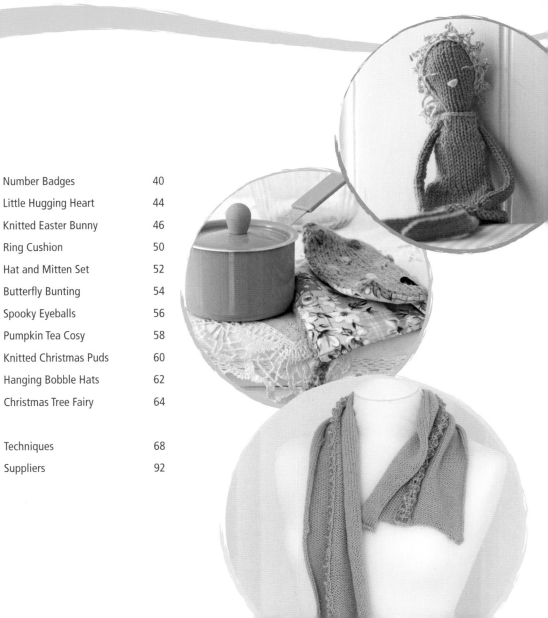

# Introduction

With over 600,000 readers *Prima* is a successful women's general interest magazine. Crafts are one of the most important aspects of the magazine and the free monthly pattern is as popular today as it was 27 years ago when *Prima* was first launched. The craft pages aim to please all levels of expertise and cover a wide range of crafts, including knitting, sewing, patchwork and embroidery, as well as many other creative ideas for you and your home. *Prima's* craft experts appeal to different generations and the magazine has successfully adapted to suit the current resurgence in crafting. From five minutes to five hours, *Prima's* projects satisfy makers of all ages.

*The Editor*

*Prima Magazine*

*London*

# Beaded Scarf

## by Laura Whitcher

## YOU WILL NEED:

- ✗ 4mm (US size 6) knitting needles

- ✗ Cable needle
  3 x 50g balls blue yarn
  Patons Diploma Gold DK
  Pastel Blue (06306)

- ✗ Three blue mini daisy bead packs
  Craft Time

- ✗ Blue sewing thread
  Gutermann colour 75

1. Knit the beaded scarf following the pattern below:

Using 4mm knitting needles and blue yarn, cast on 50 stitches.
**Row 1: (WS)** Knit.
**Row 2: (RS)** Purl 22sts, slip 2sts onto cable needle, leave at back, k1, k2 from cable needle, slip 1 stitch onto cable needle, leave at front, k2, knit stitch from cable needle, p22.
**Row 3:** K22sts, p1, add bead (by slipping onto the stitch using a sewing needle and blue thread), p2, add bead, p1, k22.
**Row 4:** P22, k6, p22.
**Row 5:** K22 sts, p1, add bead, p2, add bead, p1, k22
**Row 6:** P22, k6, p22.
**Row 7:** K22, p6, k22.
Repeat Rows 2–7, placing the beads in a line as you go. Continue in this way, leaving approximately 80cm (32in) for casting off.

2. To finish neatly stitch the ends into the back of the cast on/off rows. With wrong side facing, pin out the knitted scarf using glass headed pins to the correct size. Cover with a damp cloth and press gently using a steam iron.

# Starry Night Doorstop

## by Lisa Fordham

## YOU WILL NEED:

✗ 3.5mm knitting needles

✗ 2 x 50g balls black yarn
  1 x 25g ball pale yellow yarn
  1 x 25g ball silver yarn
  Patons Diploma Gold DK Black (06183), Patons Fab DK Lemon (02330) and Rowan Shimmer Silver (092)

✗ Black felt

✗ Leftover fabric for inner bag

✗ Clean sand

1. For the inner bag, cut six pieces from your fabric leftovers each measuring 15cm (6in) square. Pin four pieces right sides together in a row; machine stitch. Attach the fifth piece to make the bag bottom. Attach the top panel but leave the last edge unstitched. Turn through. and fill with clean sand; hand stitch the final edge closed.

2. Cast on 25sts and working in garter stitch, knit squares measuring 15cm (6in). Knit four in black and two in pale yellow yarn.

3. Sew the knitted panels together with black yarn, inserting the weighted bag before stitching closed. Cast on 12sts using black yarn and work in garter stitch a 15cm (6in) long strap. Cut a piece of black felt to the same size and sew the two together using a blanket stitch and black yarn.

4. Following the pattern below, knit and attach three stars:

With the pale yellow and silver yarns held together, cast on 55sts. Knit one row.

**Next row:** K4 sl1, k2tog, psso, *K8, sl1 k2tog, psso; repeat from * to last 4 sts, k4. (45sts)
**Next row:** K3, sl1, k2tog, psso, *K6, sl1 k2tog, psso; repeat from * to last 3 sts, k3. (35sts)
**Next row:** K2, sl1, k2tog, psso, *K4, sl1 k2tog, psso; repeat from * to last 2 sts, k2. (25sts)
**Next row:** K1, sl1, k2tog, psso, *K2, sl1 k2tog, psso; repeat from * to last 2 sts, K1. (15sts)
**Next:** Sl1, k2tog, psso: repeat from * to end 5sts. Cut yarn, thread through rem sts, draw tight and secure. Sew sides together.

# Cute Pocket Doll
## by Claire Garland

## YOU WILL NEED:

✗ Four 3.75mm (US size 5) double-pointed needles

✗ 1 x 50g ball pink yarn **(MC)**
1 x 100g ball blue yarn **(C)**
1 x 50g ball aqua yarn **(Dress)**
Rowan Pure Wool DK Tudor Rose (046), Patons 100% Cotton 4 Ply Sky (01702) and Patons Diploma Gold DK Aqua (06243)

✗ Toy filling

✗ Pink felt

✗ White sewing thread Gutermann colour 800

✗ Small safety pin

1. Knit the pocket doll following the pattern below:

**Head and body**
Using 3.75mm double-pointed needles and MC cast on 10sts.
**Step 1:** Hold needle with sts in left hand (LH).
**Step 2:** Hold two empty dpns parallel in right hand.
**Step 3:** Slip first stitch onto the dpn closest to you and off the LH needle. Slip next stitch onto the dpn furthest away and off the LH needle.
Repeat steps 1–3 until all 10sts are divided onto the 2 parallel dpns.
Slide sts to other end of dpns. Work in the round over two dpns using a 3rd dpn to knit with.
**Rnd 1:** Beg with the 5sts at the back, k10.
**Rnd 2:** (inc) Kf&b, k3, kf&b, kf&b, k3, kf&b. 14sts (7sts on each dpn) Place marker (small safety pin).
**Rnd 3:** K14.

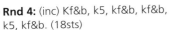

**Rnd 4:** (inc) Kf&b, k5, kf&b, kf&b, k5, kf&b. (18sts)
**Rnd 5:** K18.
Rep Rnd 5 once.
**Rnd 7:** (inc) Kf&b, k7, kf&b, kf&b, k7, kf&b. (22sts)
**Rnd 8:** K22.
Rep Rnd 8 once.
**Rnd 10:** (inc) Kf&b, k9, kf&b, kf&b, k9, kf&b. (26sts)
**Rnd 11:** K26.
Rep Rnd 11 twice.
**Rnd 14:** (dec) Sl1, k1, psso, k9, k2tog, sl1, k1, psso, k9, k2tog.
**Rnd 15:** K22.
**Rnd 16:** (dec) Sl1, k1, psso, k7, k2tog, sl1, k1, psso, k7, k2tog.
**Rnd 17, 19, 21:** K.
**Rnds 18, 20:** decrease 4sts on each rnd; decreasing 1st at beg and end on each dpn. (10sts)
Rep Rnd 21 twice.
**Rnd 24:** (inc) Kf&b, k3, kf&b, kf&b, k3, kf&b. (14sts)
**Rnd 25:** K14.
**Rnd 26:** (inc) Kf&b, k5, kf&b, kf&b, k5, kf&b. (18sts)
**Rnd 27:** K18.
Rep Rnd 27 16 times.
Stuff the head and the body.

## Legs

**Rnd 44:** (dec) K4, sl1, k1, psso, k3, k4, sl1, k1, psso, k3. (16sts)
**Rnd 45:** K4, slide next 8sts off needles onto safety pin, k4 from back needle. (8sts)
**\*Rnd 46:** K8.
Rep last rnd until leg, measures 15cm (6in)
(K2tog) 4 times. (4sts)
Cut yarn, thread end through sts.\*\*
Rejoin yarn to rem 8sts, work as Right Leg from \* to \*\*.

## Arms

Cast on 6sts, work i-cord until arm measures 11.5cm (4½in).
Sl1, k1, psso, k2, k2tog. (4sts)
Cut yarn, thread end through sts.
Sew the arms to the side of the body working a couple of sts with sewing thread to secure.

## Hair

Using yarn C, cast on 36sts.
Work in garter stitch for 2 rows.
\*Cast on 3, cast off 3, cast off 2sts. Slip st that's on RH needle onto LH\*\*, rep from \* to \*\* to last set, cast on 3, cast off 3, cast off last 2sts.
Stitch the hair evenly onto the head with sewing thread, tie extra lengths at the back into a pony tail.

### Simple dress

Using yarn Dress, cast on 34sts and divide over 3 needles; n1 – 12sts, n2 – 10sts, n3 – 12sts.
Join in the round, being careful not to twist.
Work evenly, knitting every rnd, for 12 rnds.
**Rnd 13:** (dec) (K3, sl1, k1, psso, k2tog) twice, k6, (sl1, k1, psso, k2tog, k3) twice. (26sts)
Work evenly, knitting every rnd, for 12 rnds.
**Rnd 26:** (dec) K6, sl1, k1, psso, k2tog, k6, sl1, k1, psso, k2tog, k6. (22sts)
Work evenly, knitting every rnd, for 3 rnds.
*Shape the sleeves as follows:*
**Rnd 30:** (dec) K4, cast off 4sts, k5, cast off 4sts, k3. (14sts)
**Rnd 31:** (inc) K4, backward loop (BL) cast on 4sts, k6, BL cast on 4sts, k4. (22sts)
**Rnd 32:** K22.
Cast off.

2. Dress the doll. Embroider eyes using doubled strands of white sewing thread. Make a single stitch for the eye and as the thread emerges out onto the right side of the face, snip ends as eyelashes. Cut a tiny felt triangle for the mouth and stitch onto the face with a couple of tiny stitches.

# Busy Bee Cushion

## by Louise Butt

## YOU WILL NEED:

- ✗ 3.75mm (US size 5) knitting needles

- ✗ Four 4mm (US size 6) double-pointed needles

- ✗ 3 x 100g balls yellow yarn
  1 x 50g ball black yarn
  Patons Fab DK Canary (02305)
  Patons Diploma Gold
  DK Black (06183)

**1.** Knit the cushion following the pattern below:

### Front

Cast on 110sts in yellow yarn using 3.75mm needles. Starting with a k row work 16 rows in st st.

**Place intarsia chart:** K16 then start chart. (Note: start counting the sts from the bottom right corner, these sts are in addition to the first 16 you worked at the start of the row.) Once chart is finished, cont in st st until the length of your knitting measures the same as the width. Then cast off.

### Back

Cast on 110sts in yellow yarn and work in st st until knitting measures the same length as the front. Cast off.

**2.** For the cushion edging make a length of i-cord following the pattern below:

Using two 4mm dpns and black yarn cast on 4sts. K all sts, but don't turn the needle. Instead slide all the sts to the other end of the dpn and with right side facing, pull the working yarn to give it a slight tension and k the 4sts, then slide worked sts to the end of the needle again. Cont.

**3.** Produce a tube of knitting that is long enough to fit around all four sides of the cushion.

**4.** Darn in all ends and join three sides of the cushion. Insert a cushion pad to fit, then sew the remaining side closed. Attach the i-cord to the edge using backstitch to conceal the seam.

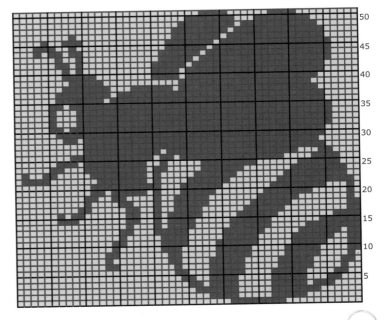

# Cute Hanging Heart
## by Dorothy Wood

## YOU WILL NEED:

✗ 4mm (US size 6)
  knitting needles

✗ 1 x 50g ball lime yarn
  Patons Dreamtime
  DK Lime (04952)

✗ Fuchsia, gold and white felt

**1.** Knit two hearts following the pattern below:

Using 4mm knitting needles and lime yarn cast on 2sts.
**Row 1: (WS)** Knit, purl to end.
**Row 2:** (RS) Increase by knitting into the front and back (kf&b) of both of the stitches on the needle. (4sts)
**Row 3:** Purl to end.
**Row 4:** Kf&b of 1st st, knit to last st, kf&b. (6sts)
**Row 5:** Purl to end.
Repeat rows 4 and 5 until 18sts.
Knit 6 rows stocking stitch.
*Knit 9 and turn, purl to end of row.
K2tog tbl, knit to last 2sts k2tog. Purl.
Repeat last 2 rows to 3sts rem, cast off knit wise on the purl side.
Rejoin yarn and work other the half of the heart from * to match.

**2.** Block the knitted hearts by lightly steam pressing on the reverse side. Using lime yarn and a blunt needle, sew together around the edges leaving a gap on a straight side. Stuff with chopped up scrap yarn or stuffing. Sew the gap closed.

**3.** Draw 2cm (¾in), 3cm (1⅛in) and 4cm (1½in) diameter circles onto three different colours of felt.

**4.** Cut out the felt circles; use pinking shears to cut out the middle circle just outside the marked line. Layer the felt onto the stuffed heart shape. Unravel some yarn and use two strands to sew through the felt and heart out the other side. Sew back through the felt. Tie at the front and trim the ends. Sew a length of yarn at the 'V' of the heart at the top. Tie the yarn ends together and trim.

# Celebration Bunting

## by Rowena Lane

## YOU WILL NEED:

✗ 4mm (US size 6)
   knitting needles

✗ 1 x 50g ball blue yarn
   1 x 50g ball red yarn
   1 x 50g ball white yarn
   Patons Diploma Gold DK
   Royal (06170), Red (06151)
   and White (06187)

✗ Satin ribbon
   (1.5cm/⅝in wide)

**1.** Make as many bunting flags as you require following the pattern below and making an equal number from each colour yarn.

Make a slip knot and place on LH needle.
**Row 1:** (RS) Increase by knitting into the front and back (kf&b) of slip knot. (2sts)
**Row 2:** Sl1, kf&b. (3sts)
**Row 3:** Sl1, kf&b, k1. (4sts)
**Row 4:** Sl1, kf&b, k2. (5sts)
**Row 5:** Sl1, kf&b, knit to end. (6sts) Repeat row 5 until 12sts on needle.
Knit 2 rows.
**Rows 14–15:** As row 5.
**Rows 16–17:** Sl1, knit to end.
**Repeat last 4 rows until 33sts on needle.**
Knit 3 rows.

**Make buttonholes:**
**Row 37:** K3 (cast off 3, k4) to end.
**Row 38:** K2 (inc in next st, yarn over, inc in next st, k3) repeat to end.
Knit 3 rows.
Cast off.

**2.** Lay out the bunting flags in a row. Stitch the top 1cm (³⁄₈in) of the outside edges of the flags together to form a continuous length. Thread ribbon through the buttonholes, leaving approximately 30cm (12in) at each end for hanging.

# Kitten Mittens

## by Claire Garland

## YOU WILL NEED:

- ✗ Four 5mm (US size 8) double-pointed needles

- ✗ 1 x 100g ball pink yarn
  Rowan Cocoon Petal (823)

- ✗ Cream, emerald green, lilac, grey and black stranded cotton (floss)
  DMC colours 726, 562, 341, 415 and 310

- ✗ Mini blue bows
  Modern Retro

**1.** Knit the mittens following the knitting pattern below:

Cast on 28sts and divide over 3 needles; n1 – 9sts, n2 – 10sts, n3 – 9sts.
Join in the round, being careful not to twist.
Work evenly, knitting every rnd, for 18 rnds.
**For right-hand mitten:** K10sts, place stitch marker – this marker tallies with the marker on the motif chart – k18.
**For left-hand mitten:** K24sts, place stitch marker – this marker tallies with the marker on the motif chart – k4
Divide for thumb.
**Rnd 20:** K18, knit into front and back of next st (kf&b), K1, kf&b, k26. (30sts)
**Rnd 21:** K30.
**Rnd 22:** Place row marker, kf&b, k4, kf&b, place row marker, k26. (32sts)
**Rnd 23:** K32.
**Rnd 24:** kf&b, k6, kf&b, k26. (34sts)
**Rnd 25:** K34.
**Rnds 26–32:** Cont to increase on every alternate round at beg of thumb (after first row marker) and end of thumb (before second

row marker), until the thumb has 16 sts. (42sts)
**Rnd 33:** K16, slide last 16 (these are the thumb sts) onto a spare length of yarn. K26.
Divide remaining stitches evenly onto 3 needles and work 1 round, leaving thumb stitches on spare yarn.
Work 4 rnds k1, p1 rib.
Cast off in rib. Weave in the end.
Rejoin 16 thumb sts to needles, dividing over 3 needles. Pick up one st at beg of thumb sts, k16, pick up 2 sts along hand junction, join in rnd as before. (19sts)

Work 3 rnds st st. Cast off.
Following the chart, work the motif using Swiss darning beginning from the marker position (red cross) and using the stranded cotton threaded in a blunt needle.
Stick then sew on a mini blue bow at the neck of the kitten motif.

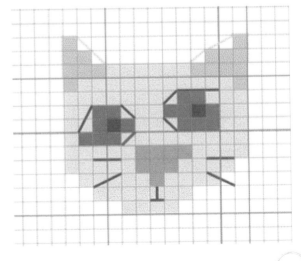

# iPad Cosy

### by Rowena Lane

## YOU WILL NEED:

✗ 5mm (US size 8) knitting needles

✗ 1 x 100g ball blue yarn (MC)
1 x 100g ball variegated yarn (C)
Rowan Cocoon Misty Blue (827) and Patons Fab DK Rainbow (02085)

✗ Button

**1.** Knit the cosy following the pattern below:

## Back

Cast on 32sts in MC.
**Row 1:** K4, p4 to end.
**Row 2:** P4, k4 to end.
Repeat Rows 1 and 2 three times (6 rows worked).
**Row 7:** P4, k4 to end.
**Row 8:** K4, p4 to end.
Repeat rows 7 and 8 three more times.
These 12 rows form the pattern. Rep until work measures 27cm (10⅝in).

### Shape flap:

**Row 1:** K1, K2tog, k to last 3sts, K2tbl, K1.
**Row 2:** K to end of row.
Repeat rows 1and 2 three times. (26sts)
Change to yarn C and continue decreasing on alternate rows as above for next 4 rows.
Change back to MC (use doubled) and cont in patt until 10sts rem on needle. K next row.

### Make buttonhole:

**Row 1:** K3, cast off 4sts, knit to end.
**Row 2:** K3, Yfwd, K3. (7sts)
**Row 3:** Knit to end.
**Row 4:** K1, K2tog, K1, K2tog tbl, K1. (5sts)
**Row 5:** Knit to end.
**Row 6:** K1, K3tog, K1. (3sts)
Cast off.

### Front

Using yarn C, cast on 32sts. Work as for back until 24cm (9½in) long.
Next rows k to end, until work measures 27cm (10⅝in).

Cast off.

**2.** Stitch the front onto the back to make the pouch.
Fold the flap over the front, mark the button position, then sew the button on.

# Camera Book Cover

## by Louise Butt

## YOU WILL NEED:

✗ 3.75mm (US size 5) knitting needles

✗ 2 x 50g balls black yarn 1 x 50g ball white yarn
Patons Diploma Gold DK Black (06183) and White (06187)

1. Knit the photograph album book cover following the pattern below:

Using 3.75mm needles and black yarn, cast on 90sts and work 4 rows garter stitch.

**Row 1:** K.

**Row 2:** K6, p to last 6sts, k6. (Work these 2 rows throughout while including the chart, to give you a flat selvedge.)

Work a further 6 rows in black.

**Place intarsia chart:** Work 20sts, then place chart. (Note: start counting the sts from the bottom right corner, these sts are in addition to the first 20 you worked at the start of the row.) Once chart is complete, continue with Rows 1 and 2 until knitting from last row of garter stitch measures 21cm (8¼in). Work 4 rows garter stitch. Cast off.

2. With wrong side facing, pin out the knitted panel using glass headed pins to the correct size. Cover with a damp cloth and press gently using a steam iron. With the wrong side of your work facing you, fold over each edge by 4cm (1½in) and join using backstitch above the bottom section of garter stitch and below the top section of garter stitch. Insert your photograph album.

# Polka Dot Pan Holder

## by Claire Garland

### YOU WILL NEED:

- ✗ 1 x ball grey aran yarn - MC
- ✗ Small amounts DK yarn for the polka dots - CC
- ✗ 7mm (US size 10½) knitting needles
- ✗ 5.00mm (US size 8/H) crochet hook
- ✗ Vintage fabric, 22 x 22cm (8½ x 8½in)
- ✗ Wool felt, 20 x 20cm (8 x 8in)

1. Tension 15 sts x 16.5 rows = 10 cm in stocking stitch an holder

md – make dot – knit into front, knit into back, knit into front of next stitch (3sts yarn CC on RH needle) turn, p3 tog, turn, k1

In MC – Cast on 30sts.
Work st st for 4 rows.
**Row 5** MC – k2, [CC –md, MC – k5] 4 times, CC – md, MC – k3.
Cut yarn CC at end of row.
St st 5 rows.
**Row 11** [MC – k5, CC –md] 4 times, CC – md, MC – k6.
St st 5 rows.
Rep last 12 rows (Rows 5 – 16) once.
**Row 29** as row 5
End with 4 rows st st .
Cast off k-wise. Weave in all stray ends.

2. Attach yarn MC and CC held together to one of the corners and work 16CH. Join with slip stitch in base of first ch. Weave in ends. If necessary lightly steam and re shape into a square shape – using the felt square as a guide.

3. Using the felt square as a guide press a 1cm (½in) hem all round the fabric square to wrong sides. Wrong sides together pin, then whip-stitch the fabric to the knitted panel with the felt square sandwiched in between.

# Snake Scarf

## by Zoe Larkins

## YOU WILL NEED:

- ✗ 8mm (US size 11) knitting needles
- ✗ 2 x 100g balls variegated yarn
  Rowan Colourscape Chunky Ghost (435)
- ✗ Red, white and black felt
- ✗ Violet ribbon
- ✗ Toy filling

**1.** Cast on 20sts using 8mm needles working in stocking stitch (one row knit, one row purl) until required length is achieved.

**2.** When you have reached the desired length for your scarf, start decreasing your stitches following the pattern below:

**Row 1:** K3, K2tog tbl, K2tog, K6, K2tog, K2tog tbl, K to end. (16sts)
**Row 2:** Purl to end.
**Row 3:** K2, K2tog tbl, K2tog, K4, K2tog, K2tog tbl, K to end. (12sts)
**Row 4:** As row 2.
**Row 5:** K1, K2tog tbl, K2tog, K6, K2tog, K2tog tbl, K to end. (8sts)

**Row 6:** As row 2.
**Row 7:** K1, Sl1, K2tog, psso, Sl2 knitwise, K1, psso, K1. (4sts)
**Row 8:** As row 2
**Row 9:** K1, P2tog, K1. (3sts)
**Row 10:** K3tog. (1sts)
Break off yarn and pull through. Sew up the sides of the scarf from the tail end, as though you are making a tube.

**3.** Approximately 20cm (8in) from the end, stop and stitch around the tube to gather in and make your snake's 'neck'.

**4.** Stitch from the head to the neck, leaving you with a pocket that you will fill with the toy filling.

**5.** Once the snake's head is firmly filled, stitch the gap closed. Attach some felt circle eyes cut from white and black felt. Cut a tongue from red felt and stitch in place. Tie a smart ribbon bow around the snake's neck to finish.

# Stripey Bling Cushion
## by Jo Irving

## YOU WILL NEED:

✗ 3.25mm (US size 3) knitting needles

✗ 1 x 100g ball green yarn **(MC)** 1 x 25g ball purple yarn **(C)**
Patons 100% Cotton 4 Ply Apple (01205) and Rowan Kidsilk Haze Blackcurrant (641)

✗ Fabric for cushion back: One piece 50cm x 50cm (20in x 20in)
Liberty Art Mayfair Mosaic Flower Blue

✗ Green sewing thread Gutermann colour 582

1. Divide the kid silk haze (yarn C) into two separate balls to make it easier for you to knit with two threads of this fine yarn.

2. Knit the cushion front following the pattern below:

Using yarn MC cast on 105sts (thumb method) and starting with a knit row knit st st (knit on right side RS, purl on wrong side WS) for 10 rows.
**Row 11:** Using two strands of yarn C, knit one row.
**Row 12:** Yarn MC for 8 rows.
**Row 20:** Yarn C for 2 rows.
**Row 22:** Yarn MC for 8 rows.
**Row 30:** Yarn C for 3 rows.
**Row 33:** Yarn MC for 8 rows.
**Row 41:** Yarn C for 4 rows.
Repeat this pattern until your knitted piece measures the size of your cushion pad (approximately 46cm x 46cm/18in x 18in). Cast off and sew in the loose yarn ends.

3. Press your fabric square and carefully press your knitted square. With right sides facing, sew the knitted square to the fabric leaving one edge open.

4. Slip the cushion cover over the cushion pad. Over sew the open seam to join the knitted and fabric edge, leaving a neat seam.

# Knitted Charms

## by Claire Garland

## YOU WILL NEED:

✗ Four 3mm (US size 2) double-pointed needles

✗ 1 x 100g ball yellow yarn (A)
  1 x 50g ball pink yarn (B)
  1 x 50g ball red yarn (C)
  1 x 50g ball purple yarn (D)
  1 x 50g ball white yarn (E)
  Rowan Creative Focus Worsted Saffron (03810), Rowan Pure Yarn DK Hyacinth (026), Rowan Baby Alpaca DK Cherry (224), Rowan Baby Alpaca DK Blossom (225) and Rowan Purelife British Sheep Breeds DK Bluefaced Leicester (780)

✗ Blue felt

✗ White sewing thread Gutermann colour 800

✗ Row marker

✗ Toy filling

✗ Buttons (optional)

1. Knit the bird, flower and heart charms following the patterns below. (Note: the charms use only very small amounts of yarn so you will have plenty to make several of each if you choose to.

## Bird charm:

In yarn E cast on 8sts.
**\*Step 1:** Hold needle with sts in left hand (LH).
**Step 2:** Hold 2 empty dpns parallel in right hand.
**Step 3:** Slip 1st stitch onto the dpn closest to you and off the LH needle. Slip next stitch onto the dpn furthest away and off the LH needle. \*\*
Repeat Steps 1–3 until all 8sts are divided onto the 2 parallel dpns. Slide sts to other end of dpns. Work in the round over 2 dpns using a 3rd dpn to knit with.
**Rnd 1:** Beg with the 4sts at the back, k8.
**Rnd 2:** (inc) Kf&b, k2, kf&b, kf&b, k2, kf&b. (12sts – 6sts on each dpn)
**Rnds 3, 5, 7, 9:** K.
**Rnds 4, 6, 8:** Increase 4sts on each rnd; increasing 1st at beg and end on each dpn. (24sts)
**Rnd 10:** (inc) Kf&b, k11, k11, kf&b. (26sts)
**Rnd 11:** (inc) Kf&b, k11, kf&b, kf&b, k11, kf&b. (30sts)
**Rnd 12:** (inc) Kf&b, k14, k14, kf&b. (32sts)
**Rnd 13:** (inc) Kf&b, k15, k15, kf&b. (34sts)
**Rnd 14:** (inc) Kf&b, k14, k2tog, k2tog, k14, kf&b.
Rep last round once.
Cut yarn leaving a 23cm (9in) length.

## Making up

Very lightly stuff the little bird with toy filling or scrap yarn. Graft to join.
Cut an equilateral triangle (approximately 1.3cm/½in each side) from blue felt for the beak, fold in half, point to point, and sew on with the two halves touching the bird (the fold becomes the top of the beak). Cut a 2.5cm (1in) diameter circle then cut the circle in half for the wings and oversew the straight edge onto the sides of the bird's body. Sew a stitch or two using a length of contrasting yarn for the eyes.

## Flower charm:
### Double petal

In yarn A cast on 6sts.
Divide over 2 dpns as Bird Charm from \* to \*\*.

Repeat Steps 1–3 until all 6sts are divided onto the 2 parallel dpns. Slide sts to other end of dpns. Work in the round over two dpns using a 3rd dpn to knit with.
**Rnd 1:** (inc) Beg with the 3sts at the back, *kf&b, k1, kf&b, kf&b, k1, kf&b. (10sts)
**Rnd 2:** K10.
**Rnd 3:** (inc) Kf&b, k3, kf&b, kf&b, k3, kf&b. (14sts)
**Rnd 4:** K14. Place marker.
Rep last rnd 7 times.
**Rnd 12:** (dec) Sl1, k1, psso, k3, k2tog, sl1, k1, psso, k3, k2tog. (10sts)
Stuff petal with toy filling or scrap yarn.
**Rnd 13:** (dec) Sl1, k1, psso, k1, k2tog, sl1, k1, psso, k1, k2tog. (6sts) **
**Rnd 14:** K6.
Rep last rnd three times.
Rep from * to ** (Rnds 1 – 13) once.
Cut yarn leaving a 10cm (3⅞in) length.
Graft to join.

**Flower centre**
In yarn B cast on 6sts.
Divide over 2 dpns as Bird Charm from * to **.
Continue to make as Flower Charm Petals up to Rnd 13 (at **)
Cut yarn leaving a 10cm (3⅞in) length.
Graft to join.
Make 2 more double petals. Stack all 3 double petals on top of each other and push a threaded yarn needle through the centres to join, work a few stitches to secure the stack then sew the flower centre to the middle of the stack. Splay the petals outwards to form the flower.

**Heart charm:**
In yarn C cast on 4 sts. Divide over 2 dpns as Bird Charm from * to **.
**Row 3:** Repeat Steps 1–3 until all 4sts are divided onto the 2 parallel dpns. Slide sts to other end of dpns.
Work in the round over 2 dpns

using a 3rd dpn to knit with.
**Rnd 1:** (inc) Beg with the 2sts at the back, kf&b 4 times. (8sts)
**Rnd 2:** K8.
**Rnd 3:** (inc) Kf&b, k2, kf&b, kf&b, k2, kf&b. (12sts)
**Rnds 4, 6, 8, 10, 12:** K.
**Rnds 5, 7, 9, 11:** Increase 4sts on each rnd; increasing 1st at beg and end on each dpn. (28sts)
**Rnds 13, 14:** K.
**Rnd 15:** K7, slip next 14sts off needles and onto a length of spare yarn, knit next 7.
**Rnd 16:** (dec) *Sl1, k1, psso, k3, k2tog, sl1, k1, psso, k3, k2tog. (10sts)
**Rnd 17:** K10.
**Rnd 18:** (dec) Sl1, k1, psso, k1, k2tog, sl1, k1, psso, k1, k2tog. (6sts)
Cut yarn leaving a 10cm (3⅞in) length.
Graft to join. **

## Making up

Very lightly stuff the heart with
toy filling or scrap yarn.
Divide 14sts from other side of
heart equally over 2 needles,
rejoin yarn, K14 then knit from *
to ** (Rnds 16 to end of pattern),
completing the stuffing just
before joining.
If there is a tiny gap between the
two bumps work a little stitch to
close.

2.  Join the charms together
with spare lengths of yarn or thin
ribbon, separating the charms
with buttons if you wish.

# Pretty Peg Bag

## by Louise Butt

**1.** Knit the peg bag following the pattern below:

Using 3.75mm knitting needles cast on 70sts in dark blue yarn and work 6 rows garter stitch.

### Start moss stitch
**Row 1:** (K1, p1) to end of row.
**Row 2:** (P1, k1) to end of row.
Rep these two rows until knitting measures 9cm (3½in) ending with Row 2.
**Next row:** Work moss stitch for 34sts, yarn over needle, k2tog, moss st to end of row.
Continue in moss st until knitting measures 40cm (15½in). Place row marker and work 12 rows more of moss stitch.
### Place intarsia chart:
Note: all sts of chart (even those represented by white squares) are worked in st st, with a moss st border either side. There is a 5 row border of st st above and below the peg image.
Work 13sts in moss stitch, P across the first 44sts of the chart, moss stitch to end. This is row 1 of the chart.

Once you have finished the chart including the 5-row st st border above the last row of the peg image, work 12 rows of moss stitch.
Then work 6 rows of garter stitch. Cast off.

**2.** Embroider the peg spring using backstitch, then gently press the chart area on the reverse of the knitting. Darn in all ends.

**3.** With right sides facing join the cast on and cast off edges by 7.5cm (3in) on each side.

Fold the bag so that the hanger opening is situated on the top fold. Smooth the peg bag flat and then sew along both selvedges. Turn right side out and insert coat hanger.

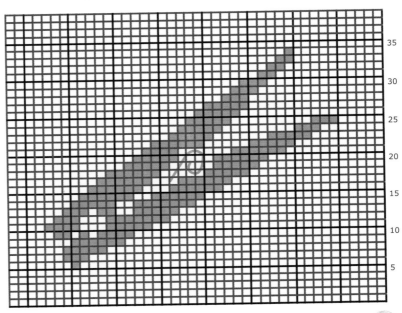

# Kindle Case

## by Lisa Fordham

### YOU WILL NEED:

- ✗ 3.5mm (US size 4) knitting needles

- ✗ 2 x 50g balls dark purple yarn (MC)
  1 x 50g ball pink yarn (C)
  Patons Diploma Gold DK Charcoal (06298) and Cyclamen (06123)

- ✗ Pink felt

- ✗ Two square buttons

**1.** Knit the case following the pattern below:

### Front

Cast on 23sts in MC yarn. Start moss stitch:
**Row 1:** (K1, p1) to end of row.
**Row 2:** As row 1.
Work 12 rows in pattern.
Change to C yarn and work 8 rows.
Change back to main colour and work until knitting measures 14cm (5½in). Cast off.

### Back

Cast on 23sts in MC yarn and work in moss stitch until back measures 24cm (9½in) to allow for flap. Cast off.

**2.** Make a lining from pink felt to match the size of the knitted cover.

**3.** Place lining inside the knitted cover and finish by using blanket stitch to attach the lining to the inside of the flap.

**4.** Attach the buttons to the front and make two small holes in the flap for the buttonholes. Blanket stitch around the buttonholes to give a clean edge.

# Number Badges

## by Claire Garland

### YOU WILL NEED:

✗ Set 3.5mm (US size 4) double-pointed needles

✗ Small amount of Rowan Creative Focus Worsted in your chosen colour

✗ Flat button 2.5cm (1in) diameter

✗ Large safety pin

✗ Scraps of brightly coloured felt

1. Knit the button cover following the pattern below:

Cast on 6sts onto one needle then complete the cast on as follows:
**Step 1:** Hold needle with sts in LH.
**Step 2:** Hold 2 empty dpns parallel in RH.
**Step 3:** Slip 1st cast on st purlwise onto the dpn closest to you and off the needle in the LH, then slip the next cast on st onto the dpn furthest away and off the RH needle.
Repeat step 3 until all 6sts are divided onto the 2 parallel dpns, 3sts on the front dpn and 3sts on the back
Slide sts to the other ends of the dpns, working yarn at back.
RS facing, cont working in the rnd, beg by knitting the sts on the back dpn – work sts over 2 dpns, using a 3rd dpn to knit with:

**Rnd 1:** (inc) Kf&b, k1, kf&b, kf&b, k1, kf&b. 10sts (5sts on each needle). Place marker.
**Rnds 2, 4, 6, 7:** K.
**Rnd 3:** (inc) Kf&b, k3, kf&b, kf&b, k3, kf&b. 14sts
**Rnd 5:** (inc) Kf&b, k5, kf&b, kf&b, k5, kf&b. 18sts
**Rnd 8:** (dec) Sl1, kl, psso, k5, k2tog, sl1, kl, psso, k5, k2tog. 14sts
**Rnd 9:** K14.
**Rnd 10:** (dec) Sl1, kl, psso, k3, k2tog, sl1, kl, psso, k3, k2tog. 10sts
Ease button into the knitted cover.
**Rnd 11:** K10.
**Rnd 12:** (dec) Sl1, kl, psso, k1, k2tog, sl1, kl, psso, k1, k2tog. 6sts

2. Cut the yarn leaving a 10cm (4in) tail. Close the opening using the grafting technique.

3. Felt the badge: soak with hot water, rub in hand soap, rinse out soap, squeeze out water, and rub until yarn is matted together to give you the felted look you are after – if the badge is still very damp, rub it in between a tea towel. Keep checking the badge for shape as you rub, re-moulding it to make the edges perfectly round. Re-shape the badge one last time before placing it on a radiator to dry.

4. Once the badge has completely dried, sew the safety pin to its reverse. Now add a felt number to the front. Using the number templates as a guide, copy your chosen number onto a piece of felt and cut out. Sew in place by working horizontal stitches around the edge of the number.

## Number badges templates

Use these full-size number templates to make personalised badges for any occasion. Alternatively, use these templates to add extra detail and embellishment to other knitting designs.

4 5 6 7

8 9 0

# Little Hugging Heart

## by Claire Garland

1. Knit the hugging heart following the pattern below:

## Arm

*Cast on 8sts onto one needle.
**Step 1:** Hold needle with sts in left hand.
**Step 2:** Hold 2 empty dpns parallel in right hand.
**Step 3:** Slip 1st cast on st purlwise onto the dpn closest to you and off the needle in the left hand, then slip the next cast on st onto the dpn furthest away and off the RH needle. **
Repeat step 3 until all 8 sts are divided onto the 2 parallel dpns, 4sts on the front dpn and 4sts on the back.
Slide sts to the other ends of the dpns, working yarn at back.
RS facing, cont working in the rnd, beginning by knitting the sts on the back dpn – work sts over 2 dpns, using a 3rd dpn to knit with:
**Rnd 1:** K8. Place marker.
Rep last rnd 14 times. Cast off.
***
Knit the other arm as before from * to ***.

### Heart

Cast on 4 sts. Cast on as Arm from * to **.

Repeat step 3 until all 4 sts are divided onto the 2 parallel dpns. Slide sts to other end of dpns. Work in the round.
**Rnd 1:** (inc) Beg with the 2sts at the back, kf&b 4 times. 8sts
**Rnd 2:** K8.
**Rnd 3:** (inc) Kf&b, k2, kf&b, kf&b, k2, kf&b. 12sts
**Rnds 4, 6, 8, 10, 12:** K.
**Rnds 5, 7, 9, 11:** Increase 4sts on each rnd; increasing 1st at beg and at end on each dpn. 28sts
**Rnds 13, 14:** K.
**Rnd 15:** K7, slip next 14sts off needles and onto a length of spare yarn, knit next 7sts.
**Rnd 16:** (dec) *Sl1, k1, psso, k3, k2tog, sl1, k1, psso, k3, k2tog. 10sts
**Rnd 17:** K10.
**Rnd 18:** (dec) Sl1, k1, psso, k1, k2tog, sl1, k1, psso, k1, k2tog. 6sts**
Cut yarn leaving a 10cm (4in) length. Join using the grafting technique.
Very lightly stuff the heart with the toy filling.
Divide 14sts from other side of heart equally over 2 needles, rejoin yarn, k14 then knit from * to ** (Rnd 16 to end of pattern), completing the stuffing just before joining.

If there is a tiny gap in between the two bumps of the heart work a little stitch to close.

2. To felt the heart and the arms, soak in hot water, then rub in a little hand soap. Wash out the soap then squeeze out the water. Rub them between your hands: the yarn will matt together to give you a felted look. Keep checking the heart for shape and re-moulding if necessary. Continue rubbing until the heart and arms are well felted, re-shaping one last time before placing on a radiator to dry.

3. Once the pieces have dried, sew the arms onto the heart with a matching thread. Sew on the two buttons for the eyes using offcuts of the yarn and work a couple of long stitches with black sewing thread for the mouth.

# Knitted Easter Bunny

## by Claire Garland

1.   Knit the bunny following the pattern below:

## Ears

*For the first ear:*

*Cast on 6sts onto one needle then complete the cast on as follows:

**Step 1:** Hold needle with sts in LH.

**Step 2:** Hold 2 empty dpns parallel in RH.

**Step 3:** Slip 1st cast on st purlwise onto the dpn closest to you and off the needle in the LH, then slip the next cast on st onto the dpn furthest away and off the RH needle.

Repeat step 3 until all 6sts are divided onto the 2 parallel dpns, 3sts on front dpn and 3sts on back.

Slide sts to the other ends of the dpns, working yarn at back.

RS facing, cont working in the rnd, beginning by knitting the sts on the back dpn – work sts over 2 dpns, using a 3rd dpn to knit with:

**Rnd 1:** K6.

Rep last rnd 14 times.**

Break yarn and leave sts on needles.

*For the second ear:*

Work as first ear from * to **.

*To join both ears:*

**Rnd 16:** K3 across front of second ear, k3 across front of first ear – all onto one dpn, k3 across back of first ear, k3 across back of second ear – all onto a second dpn. 12sts

## Begin head

**Rnd 17:** (inc) Kf&b, k4, kf&b, kf&b, k4, kf&b. 16sts (8sts each needle)

Place marker.

**Rnd 18:** K16.

**Rnd 19:** (inc) Kf&b, k3, m1, k3, kf&b (across the front of the head), kf&b, k6, kf&b (across the back of the head). 21sts

**Rnds 21, 23, 25:** K.

**Rnd 22:** (inc) K5, kf&b, k5, k10. 22sts

**Rnd 24:** (inc) K6, m1, k6, k10. 23sts

**Rnd 26:** (inc) K6, kf&b, k6, k10. 24sts

**Rnd 27:** K24.

Rep last rnd three times more.

## Shape chin/neck

**Rnd 31:** (dec) [Sl1, kl, psso, k2twice, k2tog, k2, k2tog, k10. 20sts

**Rnd 32:** K20.

**Rnd 33:** (dec) Sl1, kl, psso, k6, k2tog, sl1, kl, psso, k6, k2tog. 16sts

**Rnd 34:** K16.

Rep last rnd twice more.

## Shape front

**Rnd 37:** (inc) K4, m1, k4, k8. 17sts

**Rnds 38, 40, 42, 44, 46, 48, 50:** K.

**Rnd 39:** (inc) K4, kf&b, k4, k8. 18sts

**Rnd 41:** (inc) K5, m1, k5, k4, m1, k4. 20sts
**Rnd 43:** (inc) K5, kf&b, k5, k4, kf&b, k4. 22sts
**Rnd 45:** (inc) K6, m1, k6, k5, m1, k5. 24sts
**Rnd 47:** (inc) K6, kf&b, k6, k5, kf&b, k5. 26sts
**Rnd 49:** (inc) K7, m1, k7, k6, m1, k6. 28sts
**Rnd 51:** (inc) K7, kf&b, k7, k6, kf&b, k6. 30sts
**Rnd 52:** K30.
Rep last rnd 10 times.
**Rnd 63:** (dec) Sl1, kl, psso, 12, k2tog, k14. 28sts

### Legs
*First leg:*
**Rnd 64:** K7, slip the next 7sts off the needle and onto a safety pin, slip next 7 sts (from back needle) off the needle and onto another safety pin, knit next 7 sts onto a second dpn – 7sts on one needle, 7sts on the other.

Place marker.
***Rnd 65:** K14.
Rep last rnd 9 times.
*Foot:*
**Rnd 75:** (inc) K3, kf&b, k3, k7. 15sts
**Rnds 76, 78, 80:** K.
**Rnd 77:** (inc) K4, m1, k4, k7. 16sts
**Rnd 79:** (inc) K4, kf&b, k4, k7. 17sts
**Rnd 81:** (inc) K5, m1, k5, k7. 18sts
**Rnd 82:** K18.
Rep last rnd 10 times.
**Rnd 93:** (dec) Sl1, kl, psso, k7, k2tog, k7. 16sts
**Rnd 94:** K16.
**Rnd 95:** (dec) Sl1, kl, psso, k5, k2tog, k7. 14sts**
Cut yarn leaving 10cm (4in) tail. Finish seam using grafting technique.
Stuff the body, leg and foot.
*Second leg:*
Slip 2 sets of 7sts that are held on

the safety pins onto 2 dpns. With front of the bunny facing you rejoin yarn to first set of 7sts and work the second leg as the first from * to **. Stuff the leg and foot. Cut yarn leaving 10cm (4in) tail. Finish seam using grafting technique. If there is a gap between the legs, work a couple of sts to close it.

### Arms (make 2)
Leaving a long tail end (to sew the arm to the body later), cast on 8sts onto one needle then complete the cast on using the same method used for the ears.
**Rnd 1:** K8. Place marker.
Rep last rnd 10 times.
**Rnd 12:** (inc) K2, m1, k2, k4. 9sts
**Rnds 13, 15, 17, 19, 21, 23, 25, 27:** K.
**Rnd 14:** (inc) K2, kf&b, k2, k4. 10sts
**Rnd 16:** (inc) K3, m1, k3, k4. 11sts

**Rnd 18:** (inc) K3, kf&b, k3, k4. 12sts
**Rnd 20:** (inc) K4, m1, k4, k4. 13sts
**Rnd 22:** (inc) K4, kf&b, k4, k4. 14sts
**Rnd 24:** (dec) Sl1, kl, psso, k6, k2tog, k4. 12sts
**Rnd 26:** (dec) Sl1, kl, psso, k4, k2tog, k4. 10sts
**Rnd 28:** (dec) Sl1, kl, psso, k2, k2tog, k4. 8sts
Stuff the arm.
Cut yarn, thread end through rem 8sts, pull up tight and secure. Join the arms to the sides of the body using the tail ends.

2. Work the facial details. For the nose, sew a few straight lines in pink. For the mouth, sew two single straight lines in an upside down T-shape in black. To form the eyes, work a few small stitches in black, over and over, symmetrically on either side of the head.

3. Make a bobtail from cream yarn using the smaller of the pompom templates and sew in place on the back of the toy. Cut out an oval shape from gold felt and sew onto the front, working small horizontal stitches around the edge of the tummy.

# Ring Cushion

## by Louise Butt

## YOU WILL NEED:

✗ 3.25mm (US size 3) knitting needles

✗ 4mm (US size 6) knitting needles

✗ 1 x 50g ball Patons Fairytale 4 Ply in following colours: snow white and blue

✗ 3.5mm (US size E/4) crochet hook

✗ Toy filling

1. Knit the ring cushion following the pattern below:

## Back

Using 3.25mm needles and white yarn, cast on 32sts.
Work stocking stitch for 14cm (5½in).
Cast off.

## Front

Using 3.25mm needles and white yarn, cast on 32sts.
P 1 row.

**Row 1:** *cross 2 R, k4, rep from * to last 2sts, cross 2 R.

**Row 2 and all even numbered rows:** P.

**Row 3:** K1, *cross 2 L as follows miss next stitch, knit into back of 2nd st, then knit into back of both sts, slip off needle together, k2, cross 2 R, rep from * to last st, k1.

**Row 5:** K2, *cross 2 L, cross 2 R, K2, rep from * to end.

**Row 7:** K2, *k1, cross 2 R, k3, rep from * to end.

**Row 9:** K2, *cross 2 R, cross 2 L, k2, rep from * to end.

**Row 11:** K1, *cross 2 R, k2, cross 2 L, rep from * to last st, k1.

**Row 12:** P

Rep rows 1–12, until knitting measures 14cm (5½in).
Cast off.

## Border

Using 3.25mm needles and blue yarn, cast on 3sts.

**Row 1:** K.
**Row 2:** P.
**Row 3:** K1, m1, k to end.
**Row 4:** P.
**Row 5:** K1, m1, yon, K2tog, k to end
**Row 6:** P.
**Row 7:** Sl1, k1, psso, k to end.
**Row 8:** P.
**Row 9:** Sl1, k1, psso, k to end.
**Row 10:** P.

Rep from row 3 until border measures 14cm (5½in) – 5 points.

K.
P.
K.
P.
Rep from row 3 three times.
Cast off.

2. To make up the ring cushion, place the front and back together with right sides facing and with the border sandwiched in between. Sew through all three pieces of knitting to join leaving a 5cm (2in) gap for turning. Turn right side out and stuff with toy filling. Sew gap closed.

3. To make the ties, using a 3.5mm crochet hook and white yarn, crochet two 25cm (10in) chains. Attach these to the top right of the cushion with a couple of small neat hand stitches.

# Hat and Mitten Set

## by Louise Butt

## YOU WILL NEED:

- ✗ Set 3.25mm (US size 3) double-pointed needles

- ✗ 2 x 50g ball Patons Fairytale 4 Ply shade 04381

- ✗ Stitch marker

- ✗ Tapestry needle

**Note** the pattern has been given for four sizes to fit head circumferences as follows:
newborn 30cm (12in);
6-month-old 35.5cm (14in);
12-month-old 40.5cm (16in);
12–24-month-old 46cm (18in).

**1.** Cast on 90 (96, 108, 120) sts and arrange sts over 4 needles taking care not to twist the stitches, and placing a marker to show beginning and end of round. Work a k1, p1 rib for 10 rounds. K 5 rounds.

**Bobble round 1:** *K5, make bobble (MB) as follows (yon, k1) three times in next st; turn sl1, P5; turn sl1, k5; turn p2tog 3 times; turn sl1, k2tog, psso, rep from * to end of round.

**Next round:** *K5, k1tbl, rep from * to end of round.
K5 rounds.

**Bobble round 2:** K3, *(yon, k1) three times in next st; turn sl1, p5; turn sl1, k5; turn p2tog 3 times; turn sl1, k2tog, psso, k5, rep from * to last 3sts, *(yon, k1) three times in next st; turn sl1, p5; turn sl1, k5; turn p2tog 3 times; turn sl1, k2tog, psso, k2.

**Next round:** *K5, k1tbl, rep from * to end of round.
Knit every round until knitting measures: 12.5cm (14cm, 16.5cm, 18cm) [5in (5½in, 6½in, 7in)]

**Next row:** *K4, k2tog, rep from * to end. 75 (80, 90, 100) sts
**Next row:** K.

**Next row:** *K3, k2tog, rep from * to end. 60 (64, 72, 80) sts
**Next row:** K.
**Next row:** *K2, k2tog, rep from * to end. 45 (48, 54, 60) sts
**Next row:** K.
**Next row:** *K1, k2tog, rep from * to end. 30 (32, 36, 40) sts
**Next row:** K.
**Next row:** K2tog to end. 15 (16, 18, 20) sts
**Next row:** K.
**Next row:** K1 (0, 0, 0), k2tog to end. 8 (8, 9, 10) sts
Cut yarn, thread onto a tapestry needle and draw through sts, then fasten on reverse of hat. Sew in loose ends on wrong side of fabric.

**2.** Knit the mittens following the pattern below. Make 2. Cast on 24 (28, 36, 44) sts and arrange sts over 4 needles taking care not to twist the stitches, and placing a marker to show beginning and end of round.

Work k1, p1 rib until knitting measures 4cm (4cm, 5cm, 5cm) [1½in (1½in, 2in, 2in)].
**Increase round:** *K6 (7, 9, 11), m1, rep from * to end of round. 28 (32, 40, 48) sts
**Next round:** K
**Increase round:** *K7 (8, 10, 12), m1, rep from * to end of round. 32 (36, 44, 52) sts
**Next row:** MB, *k4 (5, 7, 9) MB, rep from * once more, k to end of round.
K every round until knitting measures 9cm (9cm, 11cm, 13cm) [3½in (3½in, 4½in, 5in)].
**Next round:** *K2, k2tog, rep from * to end of round. 24 (27, 33, 39) sts
**Next round:** K.
**Next round:** *K1, k2tog, rep from * to end of round. 16 (18, 22, 26) sts
**Next round:** *K2tog to end of round. 8 (9, 11, 13) sts
**Next round:** K0 (1, 1, 1), *k2tog, rep from * to end of round. 4 (5, 6, 7) sts
Cut yarn and thread through sts, pull tightly and fasten off on the wrong side.

# Butterfly Bunting

## by Claire Garland

## YOU WILL NEED:

✗ Set 5mm (US size 8) double-pointed needles

✗ 1 x 100g ball of M S Roving Wool in following colours: blue, pink, lilac and cream

✗ White, pink and grey felt

✗ Embroidery thread

✗ Pompom making set

1. Knit the bunting pennants following the pattern below:

**Cast** on 30sts onto one needle as follows:
**Step 1:** Hold needle with stitches in left hand.
**Step 2:** Hold 2 empty dpns parallel in right hand.
**Step 3:** Slip 1st cast on st purlwise onto the dpn closest to you and off the needle in the left hand, then slip the next cast on st onto the dpn furthest away and off the RH needle.
**Repeat** step 3 until all 30sts are divided onto the 2 parallel dpns, 15sts on the front dpn and 15sts on the back
**Slide** sts to the other ends of the dpns, working yarn at back. RS facing, cont working in the rnd, beg by knitting the sts on the back dpn – work sts over 2 dpns, using a 3rd dpn to knit with.
**Rnd 1:** K30. Place marker.
**Rnd 2:** (dec) K1, sl1, kl, psso, k9, k2tog, k1, k1, sl1, kl, psso, k9, k2tog, k1. 26sts (13 sts on each needle)
**Rnds 3, 5, 7, 9, 11, 13, 15:** K.
**Rnd 4:** (dec) K1, sl1, kl, psso, k7, k2tog, k1, k1, sl1, kl, psso, k7, k2tog, k1. 22sts

**Rnd 6:** (dec) K1, sl1, kl, psso, k5, k2tog, k1, k1, sl1, kl, psso, k5, k2tog, k1. 18sts
**Rnd 8:** (dec) K1, sl1, kl, psso, k3, k2tog, k1, k1, sl1, kl, psso, k3, k2tog, k1. 14sts
**Rnd 10:** (dec) K1, sl1, kl, psso, k1, k2tog, k1, k1, sl1, kl, psso, k1, k2tog, k1. 10sts
**Rnd 12:** (dec) K2, sl1, kl, psso, k1, k2, sl1, kl, psso, k1. 8sts
**Rnd 14:** (dec) [Sl1, kl, psso, k2tog] twice. 4sts
**Rnd 16:** (dec) Sl1, kl, psso, k2tog. 2sts
Cut yarn, thread end through rem 2sts, pull up tight and secure end.

2. To felt the pennants, soak in hot water, then rub in a little hand soap. Wash out the soap and squeeze out the water. Rub each pennant between your hands: the yarn will matt together to give you a felted look. Keep checking the pennant for shape and re-moulding if necessary. Continue rubbing until the pennant is quite dry and well felted, re-shaping one last time before placing on a radiator to dry.

3. Make medium-sized pompoms from coloured yarn to finish each pennant and sew to the base of each pennant (opposite the cast on edge).

4. Use the template to cut butterflies from the felt, one for each pennant. To sew the butterflies on work straight stitches through the middle of the butterfly to make the body, then stitch two long stitches onto the knitted fabric for the antennae.

5. To join the pennants simply thread the desired length of yarn through the cast on edge of each pennant leaving enough yarn at each end for hanging.

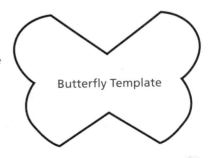

Butterfly Template

# Spooky Eyeballs

## by Claire Garland

## YOU WILL NEED:

✗ Set 3.5mm (US size 4) double-pointed needles

✗ 1 x 25g ball Patons Fab DK acrylic yarn cream

✗ Toy filling

✗ Red sewing thread

✗ 1.8cm (¾in) diameter toy eye with plastic washer

1. Knit the eyeball following the pattern below:

Cast on 6sts.
**Rnd 1:** K6.
Work as i-cord as follows:
Slide sts to other end of needle without turning. Keeping gauge tight, pull working yarn across the back of the i-cord.
**Rnd 2:** (inc) [Kf&b] 6 times. 12sts
**Rnd 3:** Divide 12sts evenly over 3 dpns, 4sts on each needle. K. With righ side facing and keeping the gauge fairly tight on the first round, work in the round as follows:
**Rnd 4:** (inc) [K1, kf&b] 6 times. 18sts
**Rnds 5, 7, 9, 11:** K.
**Rnd 6:** (inc) [K2, kf&b] 6 times. 24sts
**Rnd 8:** (inc) [K3, kf&b] 6 times. 30sts

**Rnd 10:** (inc) [K4, kf&b] 6 times. 36sts
**Rnd 12:** (dec) [K4, k2tog] 6 times. 30sts
**Rnds 13, 15, 17, 19:** K.
**Rnd 14:** (dec) [K3, k2tog] 6 times. 24sts
**Rnd 16:** (dec) [K2, k2tog] 6 times. 18sts
**Rnd 18:** (dec) [K1, k2tog] 6 times. 12sts
Fit in the toy eye and stuff with the toy filling.
**Rnd 20:** (dec) [K2tog] 6 times. 6sts
Cut yarn, thread end through the remaining 6sts, pull up tight and secure the end.

2. Sew a few lines through the yarn with the red thread to create the bloodshot effect.

# Pumpkin Tea Cosy

## by Claire Garland

## YOU WILL NEED:

✗ 5mm (US size 8) knitting needles

✗ 1 x 100g ball Rowan Creative Focus Worsted in following colours: orange (A) and green (B)

✗ White and brown yarn

**1.** Knit the tea cosy following the pattern below:

### Sides (make 2)
Cast on 40 sts.
**Row 1 (RS):** Using A, [K6, p2] 5 times.
**Row 2** Using A, [k2, p6] 5 times.
Rows 1 and 2 form patt.
Cont in patt (Row 2) until side measures 15cm (6in), ending WS.

### Shape top
Keeping patt correct, cont as follows:
**Next row (RS):** (dec) K6, p2tog, rep from * to end. 35sts
**Next row:** *K1, p6, rep from * to end.
**Next row:** (dec) K5, p2tog, rep from * to end. 30sts

**Next row:** (dec) P4, k2tog, rep from * to end. 25sts
**Next row:** (dec) K3, p2tog, rep from * to end. 20sts
**Next row:** (dec) P2, k2tog, rep from * to end. 15sts

### Stalk
Change to yarn B.
**Next row:** *K1, p1, rep from * to last stitch, k1.
**Next row:** *P1, k1, rep from * to last stitch, p1.
Rep last 2 rows twice.
**Next row:** (dec) *K1, p2tog, rep from * to end. 10sts
**Next row:** *K1, p1, rep from * to end.
**Next row:** (dec) K2tog 5 times. 5sts.
Cast off.

**2.** Join sides leaving spout and handle openings. Embroider face using the photograph as a guide.

# Knitted Christmas Puds

## by Claire Garland

## YOU WILL NEED:

- ✗ Set 2.5mm (US size 1) double-pointed needles
- ✗ 3mm (US size C/2) crochet hook
- ✗ 1 x 50g ball Rowan Felted Tweed DK brown (A)
- ✗ 1 x 25g ball Patons Fab DK Acrylic Yarn cream (B)
- ✗ Toy filling
- ✗ Green felt
- ✗ Red sewing thread

**1.** Knit the Christmas puddings following the pattern below:

Using 2.5mm double-pointed needles and yarn A, cast on 6sts and knit one row as follows: k6, slide sts to the top end/other end of the dpn bring working yarn around back – across sts at the back – and k6 across the front.
Divide sts, slip purl-wise, equally over 3 dpns.
Place stitch marker and begin to knit in the round.
**Rnd 1:** (inc) Kf&b all sts. 12sts
**Rnds 2, 4, 6, 8, 10, 12, 13: K.**
**Rnd 3:** (inc) [K1, kf&b] 6 times. 18sts
**Rnd 5:** (inc) [K2, kf&b] 6 times. 24sts
**Rnd 7:** (inc) [K3, kf&b] 6 times. 30sts
**Rnd 9:** (inc) [K4, kf&b] 6 times. 36sts
**Rnd 11:** (inc) [K8, kf&b] 4 times. 40sts
Change to yarn B.
**Rnd 14:** K40.
**Rnd 15:** (dec) [K8, sl1, kl, psso] four times. 36sts
**Rnds 16, 18, 20, 22, 24: K.**
**Rnd 17:** (dec) [K4, sl1, kl, psso] 6 times. 30sts
**Rnd 19:** (dec) [K3, sl1, kl, psso] 6 times. 24sts
**Rnd 21:** (dec) [K2, sl1, kl, psso] 6 times. 18sts
Stuff pudding with toy filling.
**Rnd 23:** (dec) [K1, sl1, kl, psso] 6 times. 12sts
**Rnd 25:** (dec) Sl1, kl, psso 6 times. 6sts
Cut yarn, thread end through yarn needle, pass needle through rem 6sts, pull up tight to close hole, then secure the end.

**2.** To make the sauce 'drips', make 38 chain using yarn B and crochet hook. Fasten off. Wrap the chain around the pudding securing with yarn or sewing thread as you go around.

**3.** Cut out holly leaves from green felt and sew in place on top of the pudding with French knot 'berries' worked with red sewing thread.

**Holly Leaf Template**

# Hanging Bobble Hats

## by Claire Garland

## YOU WILL NEED:

✗ Set 3.5mm (US size 4) knitting needles

✗ 1 x 50g ball Rowan Baby Alpaca DK in colours of your choosing

✗ Green ric rac

✗ Pompom maker set

1. Knit the hats following the pattern below:

Cast on 36 sts. Divide evenly over 3 needles slipping purlwise, join in the round.
**Rnd 1:** [K2, P2] 9 times.
Place marker.
**Rnd 2:** P.
**Rep last 2 rnds 8 times.** Cast off in rib.

2. Take one of the knitted hat pieces and turn up the ribbed brim. Then at the cast on edge, thread up the tail end and work a running stitch all the way around. Pull up the stitches to create the hat shape, and secure the end.

3. Make small pompoms. Sew a pompom securely in place at the top of the hat to hide the stitching.

4. Sew on a loop of yarn at the top of the bobble for hanging. Thread the completed hats onto a length of ric rac to make a garland.

5. For an advent calendar, make 24 hats; embroider each with a number (1 to 24) worked with yarn, or use a marker to write the numbers onto 24 wooden pegs and attach to a length of ribbon.

# Christmas Tree Fairy

## by Claire Garland

## YOU WILL NEED:

- ✗ Set 2.5mm (US size 0) double-pointed needles

- ✗ 1 x 50g ball Patons Fairytale 4 Ply pink

- ✗ Patterned fabric for dress: Two pieces 8cm x 13cm (3⅛in x 5in)

- ✗ Sewing thread: white, blue, pale pink, gold, and colour to match patterned fabric

- ✗ White felt

- ✗ Silver glitter glue

1. Knit the fairy following the pattern below:

### Head and body

Cast on 10sts onto one needle then complete the cast on as follows:

**Step 1:** Hold needle with sts in left hand.

**Step 2:** Hold 2 empty dpns parallel in right hand.

**Step 3:** Slip 1st cast on st purlwise onto the dpn closest to you and off the needle in the left hand, then slip the next cast on st onto the dpn furthest away and off the RH needle.

Repeat step 3 until all 10 sts are divided onto the 2 parallel dpns, 5sts on the front dpn and 5sts on the back.

Slide sts to the other ends of the dpns, working yarn at back.

RS facing, cont working in the rnd, beginning by knitting the sts on the back dpn – work sts over 2 dpns, using a 3rd dpn to knit with:

**Rnd 1:** K10. Place marker.

Rep last rnd 11 times. Stuff the head.

**Rnd 13:** (dec) K2 tog, k1, sl1, kl, psso, k2 tog, k1, sl1, kl, psso. 6sts (3 sts on each needle)

**Rnds 14, 15, 17:** K.

**Rnd 16:** (inc) Kf&b, k1, kf&b, kf&b, k1, kf&b. 10sts

**Rnd 18:** (inc) Kf&b, k3, kf&b, kf&b, k3, kf&b. 14sts

**Rnd 19:** K14.

Rep last rnd 14 times.

Stuff the head and body lightly with some spare yarn or scrap of toy stuffing.

**Rnd 34:** (dec) K3, sl1, kl, psso, k2, k3, sl1, kl, psso, k2. 12sts

### Divide for legs

**Rnd 35:** K3, slip next 3sts off the needle and onto a safety pin, slip next 3sts, from back needle, off the needle and onto another safety pin, knit next 3sts onto the second needle – 3sts on one needle, 3sts on the other.

**Rnd 36:** *K6.

Rep last rnd until the leg measures approximately 10cm (4in).

**Next rnd:** (dec) K3 tog twice. 3sts Cut yarn, thread end through 3sts, pull up and secure the end.**

Slip 2 sets of 3sts which are held on the safety pins onto 2 dpns and work the second leg as the first from * to **. If there is a gap between the legs just work a couple of stitches to close it.

### Arms (make 2)

Leaving a long tail end (you will use this to sew the arm to the body later), cast on 4sts, *k4, slide sts to the top end/other end of the dpn bring working yarn around back – across sts at the back – and k4 across the front** to create an i-cord. Cont working the i-cord, from * to ** until it measures 6cm (2⅜in).

**Next rnd:** (dec) K2 tog twice. 2sts Cut yarn, thread end through 2sts, pull up and secure the end. Join the arms to the sides of the body using the tail ends.

2. Work the fairy's facial details. For the mouth, sew a tiny straight line in black sewing thread. To form the eyes, work a few small stitches in blue sewing thread over and over each other symmetrically on either side of the head. Add pale pink stitches to form the cheeks.

3. Now work the fairy's hair using the gold coloured sewing thread. Cut a few 20cm (8in) lengths of thread. Using a few lengths of thread at a time, fold in half to form a loop. Thread the four cut ends through the eye of a needle, then thread the needle through a knitted stitch at the top of the head, but do not pull the thread through fully – instead pass the needle through the loop and pull through until the loop lies flat on top of the head. Work as many strands of hair as you consider necessary.

4. To make the fairy's dress, take the two pieces of patterned fabric and place together with right sides facing. Using a 6mm (¼in) seam allowance, machine or hand stitch along the two long edges leaving a 1.3cm (½in) gap on each side 1.3cm (½in) down from the top edge for the armholes. Turn up a 6mm (¼in) hem at the bottom edge and sew in place. Press a 6mm (¼in) hem at the neck edge, then work a running stitch all the way around the edge; gather up the stitches, just enough so that you can still fit the doll's head inside the neck, then secure the thread. Turn under the raw ends at the armholes and oversew to neaten. Slip the finished dress onto the knitted fairy.

5. Use the template to cut a pair of wings from the felt. Decorate her toes and the wings with glitter glue – this will also stiffen the wings. Once the wings are dry, sew them onto the back of the fairy's dress.

# Techniques

## Yarns & Needles

This section tells you everything you need to know when selecting yarns and needles for your knitted projects.

### Fibres

One of the joys of being a knitter is being able to explore the fabulous range of yarns available today. Here is an introduction to the many choices that you may be offered when you enter a yarn store.

### Natural fibres

Natural fibres can be made from either animal or plant sources. They often feel better than synthetic fibres and take dyes extremely well, so they can offer a greater range of colours. However, they can need careful handling and often need to be washed with care, so you may prefer to choose synthetic fibres for items that have to stand up to heavy wear and frequent cleaning in the washing machine. Natural fibres are often more expensive than synthetic fibres, but they do add a touch of luxury and quality to any item.

**Alpaca** Spun from the coat of the alpaca to produce a soft and lustrous yarn that has many of the qualities of cashmere but comes at a more affordable price. Angora Fur of the Angora rabbit is soft and silky and yields a fibre that is fine with a fluffy 'halo'. Items made from angora are beautifully soft and warm and will last for many years if looked after carefully.

**Cashmere** Plucked from the downy undercoat of the Cashmere goat. The ultimate luxury yarn, it is lightweight, incredibly soft and very warm. It is usually blended with other fibres, such as wool, to produce a soft yarn at a more reasonable price.

**Cotton** Produced from part of the seed case of the cotton bush. It is a heavy fibre, very hard-wearing and available in a wide range of colours. Cotton can be mercerized to give it lustre and enables it to take brighter dyes. Matte cotton tends to be more loosely spun and is softer.

**Linen** Part of the stem of the flax plant. It is processed several times to produce a finished fibre that is stiff and crunchy with little elasticity. It is often blended with cotton to soften it, but on its own it has a better drape than cotton.

**Mohair** This fur comes from the Angora goat and kid mohair comes from young goats of up to 18 months old. The long hairs make a yarn than can be brushed or unbrushed and that is light and airy. Although mohair may be knitted up on its own, it is often blended with other wools and fibres to give it strength.

**Silk** A continuous filament secreted by the silkworm larva, which it spins around itself to form a cocoon. This cocoon is unwound and many of these fibres are spun together to form a fine, strong yarn. Silk has a wonderful lustre and is soft with a dry feel.

**Wool** Yarn spun from the fleece of a sheep. Different breeds of sheep produce different types of wool. Lambswool is the first shearing from an animal and is softer than subsequent shearings. Wool is a versatile yarn, being warm in winter and cool in summer. It knits up very well and stands up to unravelling and recycling with no loss of quality.

# Blended and synthetic fibres

Man-made yarns use substances that are not fibres originally but are made into fibres by the addition of chemicals. Synthetic yarns are durable and can be machine washed. They are often added to natural fibres to make a yarn that is cheaper and more elastic. Novelty yarns are often made from synthetic fibres. The most commonly used synthetic fibres are polyester, acrylic and polypropylene. Synthetic fibres also take dye well.

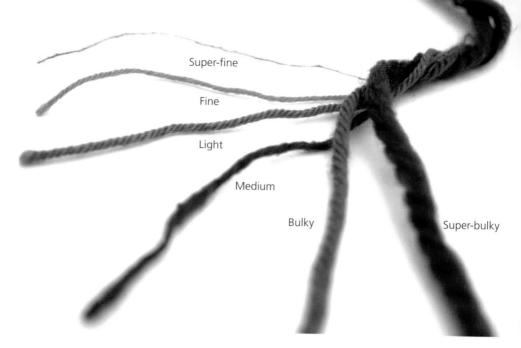

Super-fine

Fine

Light

Medium

Bulky

Super-bulky

## Weight

The weight of a yarn is its thickness, and this is how yarns are classified. Pattern stitches can look very different when they are knitted in different weights of yarn; a thin, lightweight yarn will produce a soft and delicate fabric, whereas a thick, medium weight yarn will produce a thick, heavy fabric. Why not experiment for yourself with different yarn weights to see the effects that you can get?

### TIP
When learning to knit, use a 100 per cent wool yarn; it can be unravelled and reused if needs be.

# Ply or thickness

A strand of spun yarn is called a single and plied yarn is created from singles twisted together, usually two, three or four plies. However, while the general rule is that the more plies twisted together, the thicker the yarn will be, this is not always the case because a ply could be large or small depending on the original fibre. The thickness of the yarn is also affected by the spinning process; a tightly spun ply will be thinner than a loosely spun ply.

To add to the confusion, yarn manufacturers in the US and UK sometimes use different names for the same weight of yarn. Therefore the yarn requirements described in this booklet follow the standard developed by the Craft Yarn Council of America, which divides yarns into weights rather than numbers of plies, with the common UK equivalent given in brackets. Using the chart below, you should be able to find a suitable yarn for any of the projects no matter where in the world you buy your yarn.

## STANDARD YARN WEIGHTS

| weight* | gauge* | needle size** | yarn type*** |
|---|---|---|---|
| super-fine | 27–32 sts | 1 to 3 (2.25–3.25mm) | sock, fingering (2ply, 3ply) |
| fine | 23–26 sts | 3 to 5 (3.25–3.75mm) | sport, baby (4ply) |
| light | 21–24 sts | 5 to 7 (3.75–4.5mm) | light worsted, DK (DK) |
| medium | 16–20 sts | 7 to 9 (4.5–5.5mm) | worsted, afghan (aran) |
| bulky | 12–15 sts | 9 to 11 (5.5–8mm) | chunky |
| super-bulky | 6–11 sts | 11 (8mm) and above | super-chunky |

Notes:
* Gauge (tension) is measured over 4in/10cm in stockinette (stocking) stitch
** US needle sizes are given first, with UK equivalents in brackets
*** Alternative US yarn type names are given first, with UK equivalents in brackets

TIP

Always use scissors to cut yarn. Never be tempted to break it as you will stretch the fibres.

# Colour & Texture

One of the most exciting things about knitting is the chance to experiment with colour and texture. Yarns come in many forms all of which have their own special characteristics.

**1** Self-striping yarn has long lengths of colour that slowly merge into the next colour. To heighten the effect, use two balls of yarn as you work, knitting two rows with one and two rows with the other.

**2** Ribbon yarn is a woven tape that produces a flat yarn. and it is available in many different fibres.

**3** Short-pile eyelash yarn resembles frayed ribbon. It can have short splashes of colour that merge through the texture of the yarn.

**4** Tweed yarn is a marl of two or more colours punctuated with flecks of contrasting colours.

**5** Long-pile eyelash yarn knits up into a fabric of deep, shimmering waves with randomly placed colours.

**6** Striped yarn is designed for smaller projects. In the example opposite each colour is separated by a dark blue stripe, so they are all clearly defined and do not merge with each other. Try using two balls at once, as with self-striping yarn, to break the sequence, or use two strands together to produce a marl yarn.

# Needles

There are three different types of needle:

**Straight needles** Used in pairs and have a point at one end and a fixed knob at the other. Stitches are worked using the pointed end; they cannot be removed from the other end. They are used for flat knitting, working across a row of stitches moving from one needle to the other; turning the work and working back again, and continuing back and forth.

**Double-pointed needles** These are used in sets of four or five and have a point at each end. Stitches can be worked with one end and can also be removed from the other end. This means that you don't have to turn your work at the end of each row. In fact you can continue knitting in a spiral and produce a seamless continuous tube. This is called circular knitting.

**Circular needles** These consist of a pair of needles joined by a flexible nylon wire. They have a point at each end and, like double-pointed needles, you can work from both end and so knit in rounds to produce a seamless tube.

## Needle lengths

There are three standard lengths: 10in (25cm), 12in (30cm) and 14in (35cm). Use the length appropriate to the number of stitches: stitches should fit snugly along the length of the needle, not crammed together where they can easily fall off the end.

### TIP

Invest in a needle gauge to check the size of a needle: circular and double-pointed needles tend not to be marked.

## NEEDLE SIZES

| US | Metric | US | Metric |
|----|--------|----|--------|
| 0 | 2mm | 10 | 6mm |
| 1 | 2.25mm | 10½ | 6.5mm |
| | 2.5mm | | 7mm |
| 2 | 2.75mm | | 7.5mm |
| | 3mm | 11 | 8mm |
| 3 | 3.25mm | 13 | 9mm |
| 4 | 3.5mm | 15 | 10mm |
| 5 | 3.75mm | 17 | 12.75mm |
| 6 | 4mm | 19 | 15mm |
| 7 | 4.5mm | 35 | 19mm |
| 8 | 5mm | | 20mm |
| 9 | 5.5mm | | |

## CROCHET HOOKS

| US | Metric | US | Metric |
|----|--------|----|--------|
| B1 | 2.5mm | I9 | 5.5mm |
| C2 | 2.75mm | J10 | 6mm |
| D3 | 3.25mm | K10½ | 6.5mm |
| E4 | 3.5mm | L11 | 8mm |
| F5 | 3.75mm | M/N13 | 9mm |
| G6 | 4mm | N/P15 | 10mm |
| 7 | 4.5mm | P/Q | 15mm |
| H8 | 5mm | | |

# Knitting Patterns

A knitting pattern provides you with all the instructions you need to make a project. It will tell you the type of yarn you will need, the size of needles, the gauge you need to achieve as you knit, and provide you with the instructions to make the project you have chosen.

## Gauge

Gauge (tension) is the resistance on the yarn as it passes through your fingers as you knit. Keeping a moderate, consistent and correct tension will produce an even fabric. All patterns will specify the gauge that needs to be achieved to knit the project to the correct size. It is stated as the number of stitches and rows you need to make 4in (10cm) of fabric. It is important to take time to achieve the correct gauge if you want your project to be the same size as on the pattern.

## Gauge measurement

To check your gauge, work a square of fabric that measures at least 6in (15cm) using the stated yarn, needle size and stitch. This allows you to measure the fabric in the middle of the square, away from the edges, which may be distorted.

You will not always be able to achieve both the correct stitch and row count. In these circumstances, it is more important to achieve the correct stitch count, as otherwise the item will be either too wide or not wide enough. Row count is less important as you can knit fewer or more rows to achieve the desired length if necessary. Row count becomes important when decrease instructions are given over an exact number of rows. If your row tension is not accurate, you may have to recalculate these decreases to ensure the item is the right length.

## Knitting a gauge square

Knit a gauge square in stockinette (stocking) stitch by casting on the number of stitches stated to measure 4in (10cm) plus half as many again.

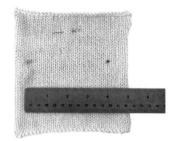

1 Work in stockinette stitch for 6in (15cm) and bind off loosely.

2 Block the square in the same way that you will the finished item.

3 Lay your square out on a flat  surface without stretching it. Using a ruler, measure and mark with a pin 1in (2.5cm) in from one edge, and then 4in (10cm) from that pin.

4   For the rows, place the ruler vertically on the square and mark the same measurements, avoiding the cast-on and bound-off edges, which may pull the fabric in.

5   Count the number of stitches and rows between the pins to get your gauge. If you have more stitches than the pattern states, your stitches are too small; try knitting the gauge square again with a size larger needle. If you have fewer stitches than the pattern states, your stitches are to big; try knitting the gauge square again with a size smaller needle.

6   Continue to adjust needle sizes and knit gauge squares until you achieve the gauge stated in the pattern.

## Measuring textured yarn

Yarn that has a lot of texture or long pile can be difficult to measure. Mark the measurements on long-pile yarns with long pieces of yarn in a contrasting colour. To make the stitches easier to see, try holding the fabric up to a window or a light. Take care to protect your eyes from strong light.

For textured yarn such as bouclé or chenille, knit sewing cotton in a contrasting colour in with the yarn as you make your square. This helps to show up the stitches. Again, mark the measurements with pieces of yarn in a contrasting colour instead of pins. This allows you to pull the fabric slightly to identify difficult stitches without the pins falling out.

If you are still having difficulty, try counting the stitches on the reverse side of the fabric – for stockinette stitch it is often easier to see the stitches on this side when using textured yarn.

## Measuring over a stitch pattern

Where the gauge is given over a stitch pattern other than stockinette stitch, cast on enough stitches to work complete repeats of the pattern. The repeat of the pattern is stated after the asterisk, so cast on a multiple of this number of stitches plus any stitches worked at the beginning and end of a row.

# Abbreviations

Abbreviations are used in knitting patterns to shorten commonly used terms so that the instructions are easier to read and a manageable length. The following is a list of the most common knitting abbreviations you need to know to make the projects featured in this booklet, many of which will be described in more detail later in this section. The green tinted box opposite lists the most common differences in US and UK knitting terms.

| | |
|---|---|
| alt | alternate |
| approx | approximately |
| beg | beginning |
| C4B | cable 4 back |
| C4F | cable 4 front |
| Cr3L | cross 3 left |
| Cr3R | cross 3 right |
| cm | centimetre(s) |
| cont | continue |
| dec(s) | decrease/decreasing |
| DK | double knitting |
| dpn | double-pointed needles |
| foll | following |
| g | gram(s) |
| g st | garter stitch (k every row) |
| inc | increase(s)/increasing |
| in(s) | inch(es) |
| k | knit |
| k2tog | knit 2 stitches together (1 stitch decreased) |
| k3tog | knit 3 stitches together (2 stitches decreased) |
| k2togtbl | knit 2 stitches together through back of loops (1 stitch decreased) |
| kf&b | knit into front and back of stitch (increase 1 stitch) |
| m | metre(s) |
| mm | millimetres |
| M1 | make one (increase 1 stitch) |
| oz | ounces |

| US TERM | UK TERM |
| --- | --- |
| stockinette stitch | stocking stitch |
| reverse stockinette stitch | reverse stocking stitch |
| seed stitch | moss stitch |
| moss stitch | double moss stitch |
| bind off | cast off |
| gauge | tension |

| | |
| --- | --- |
| p | purl |
| patt(s) | pattern(s) |
| PB | place bead |
| p2tog | purl 2 stitches together (1 stitch decreased) |
| p3tog | purl 3 stitches together (2 stitches decreased) |
| rem | remain/ing |
| rep(s) | repeat(s) |
| RS | right side |
| sk2po | slip 1 stitch, knit 2 stitches together, pass slipped stitch over (decrease 2 stitches) |
| sl | slip |
| sl2tog-k1-psso | slip 2 stitches together, knit 1 stitch, pass 2 slipped stitches over (2 stitches decreased) |
| ssk | slip 2 stitches one at a time, knit 2 slipped stitches together (1 stitch decreased) |
| st st | stockinette (stocking) stitch |
| st(s) | stitch(es) |
| tbl | through back of loop |
| tog | together |
| WS | wrong side |
| wyib | with yarn in back |
| wyif | with yarn in front |
| yd(s) | yards(s) |
| yo | yarn over |
| * | repeat directions following * as many times as indicated or end of row |
| [ ] | instructions in square brackets refer to larger sizes |
| ( ) | repeat instructions in round brackets the number of times |

# Reading a Pattern

For reasons of space, patterns use abbreviations and shorthand phrases. Many abbreviations, such as k and p, are used widely throughout all patterns. Other patterns may have specific abbreviations relating to specific stitches; these should always be explained in full at the beginning of the pattern.

# Imperial and metric measurements

The patterns give both imperial measurements (inches and ounces) and metric measurements (centimetres and grams). Make sure you stick to one set of measurements throughout your project; although most conversions are exact, there are some that are more generalized.

## COMMON SHORTHAND PHRASES

**Cont as set** This is used to avoid repeating the same instructions over and over again. Just continue to work as previously instructed. For example: Row 1 K, Row 2 P. Cont in st st as set.

**Keeping patt correct** Again, to avoid repeating instructions, this tells you to ensure you work the pattern as previously instructed, even though you have been told to do something that would otherwise interfere with the pattern. For example: Keeping centre panel pattern correct, cont in st st.

**Work as given for** This is where you are making two similar items. Instead of repeating the instructions in full as given for the first item, you are instructed to work the second item in the same way as the first item to a given point, which is usually marked by asterisks.

**Reversing all shaping** Shaping is given for one piece and the other piece must be shaped to be a mirror image of it.

* Repeat instructions following an asterisk as many times as indicated or until you reach the end of a row.
** Double asterisks usually appear at the beginning and/or end of a section of instructions which will need to be repeated.
( ) Instructions in round brackets should be repeated the indicated number of times.

## Sizes

Knitting patterns can be written in more than one size with the smallest size first (outside the brackets) and the remaining sizes inside square brackets, separated by colons. The largest size will be given at the end. Your size will always appear in the same place in the bracket; instructions for the first size will always be first, for the second size they will be second, etc. Square brackets are used to indicate the number of stitches and rows to be worked, or how many times a pattern is repeated for each size. For example, cast on 90 [92: 94: 96] sts, or work patt 1 [2: 3: 4] times. If a zero appears for your size, do not work the instructions it is referring to, for example, dec 3 [0: 1: 2] sts. If only one figure appears then it refers to all sizes.

## Working from charts

### Charts for colourwork techniques

Patterns involving the intarsia or Fair Isle colourwork techniques are worked from charts. The pattern will usually give few other instructions, except to tell you how many stitches to cast on and instructions for any parts of the project not included in the chart.

### Stitch charts

A knitting pattern may contain a stitch chart – an illustration of a cable or lace pattern or a texture pattern with each stitch being represented by a symbol, which usually reflects the texture of a stitch. A knit stitch often appears as a blank square, whilst a purl stitch is a dot or horizontal dash. The key provided alongside a stitch chart will tell you what each symbol means.

TIP: When stopping knitting make sure you mark in the pattern where you have got to.

# Casting On & Binding Off

These are the two key techniques you will need, casting on to get the yarn on to your needle ready to begin work, and binding off, removing the completed project from your needles without it unravelling.

## Casting On

To begin knitting, you need to work a foundation row of stitches and this is called casting on. There are several different ways to cast on stitches but some methods are better than others if you want to achieve certain results, so if a particular method is specified in the pattern use it.
Otherwise it is purely a matter of personal preference.

## Thumb method

This method uses only one needle and is the simplest way of casting on. Unwind a length of yarn from the ball that is enough for the number of stitches you are casting on. Allow approximately 1–1⅛ in (2.5–3cm) per stitch. Make a slip knot at this point on one needle (see The Slip Knot box opposite).

1 Hold the needle with the slip knot in your right hand. Put the ball end of the yarn over the index finger, under the middle finger and over the third finger of your right hand. Wrap the free end of the yarn around the thumb of your left hand from the back.

2 Insert the needle through the thumb loop from front to back.

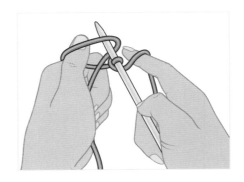

3   Using the index finger of your right hand, wrap the yarn from the ball around the needle.

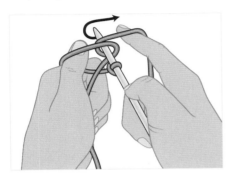

4   Pull the loop on the needle through the loop on your thumb. Slip the loop off your thumb and gently tighten the stitch up to the needle by pulling on both strands of yarn. Repeat until you have cast on the required number of stitches.

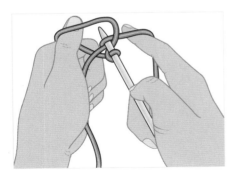

## TIP

If your casting on is always too tight, use a size larger needle. If it always too loose, use a smaller needle. But always change back to the correct size needle to begin knitting.

### THE SLIP KNOT

Follow these simple diagrams to make a slip knot, the first cast on stitch when working the thumb method cast-on. Pull the ends of the yarn to tighten it and you are ready to follow the instructions for casting on.

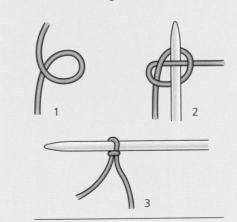

# Binding Off

Binding off (casting off) links stitches together so that they cannot unravel and secures stitches when a piece of knitting is complete. Binding off is normally done following the stitch sequence, so a knit stitch is bound off knitwise and a purl stitch purlwise. It is important not to bind off too tightly as this may pull the fabric in.

## Bind off knitwise

1 Knit the first two stitches. Insert the point of the left-hand needle into the front of the first stitch on the right-hand needle.

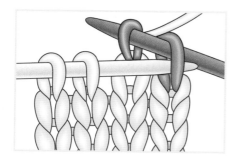

2 Lift the first stitch on the right-hand needle over the second stitch and off the needle.

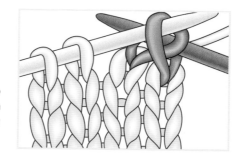

3 One stitch is left on the right-hand needle.

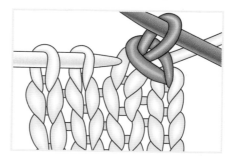

4 Knit the next stitch on the left-hand needle, so there are again two stitches on the right-hand needle. Lift the first stitch on the right-hand needle over the second stitch, as in step 2. Repeat this process until one stitch is left on the right-hand needle. Cut the yarn (leaving a length long enough to sew or weave in) and pass the end through the last stitch. Slip the stitch off the needle and pull the yarn end to tighten it.

## TIP

You will often need to leave your work without binding off. Always complete a row – finishing in the middle of a row can cause your stitches to stretch or come off the needle.

## Bind off purlwise

To bind off a purl row, all you have to do is purl the stitches instead of knitting them.

## Bind off in pattern

When you are knitting in patterns such as rib or cables, it is important to bind off in pattern to maintain an elastic edge. In this case, all that you have to do is knit the knit stitches and purl the purl stitches.

### PICKING UP STITCHES

One piece of knitting can be joined to another by picking up stitches. This eliminates a seam and makes a smoother join. Hold the work in your left hand with the right side facing. With a needle and the yarn in your right hand, insert the needle under the top of the loop of the first stitch. Wrap the yarn knitwise around the needle and draw through a loop. Continue in this way, inserting the needle under the top loop of each stitch until you have the correct number of stitches.

## TIP

Binding off too tightly can cause your fabric to pucker. This is a particular problem on a visible edge, such as on a throw. Try using a needle a size larger than that used to knit the main fabric.

# Knit & Purl

The two classic knitting stitches are the knit stitch and the purl stitch. Once you know both the knit and purl stitches, you can pretty much make anything.

## Knit Stitch

This is the simplest stitch of all and is the one that most people learn first. Each stitch is created with a four-step process. Hold the yarn at the back of the work – this is the side facing away from you.

1 Place the needle with the cast-on stitches in your left hand, insert the right-hand needle into the front of the first stitch on the left-hand needle from left to right

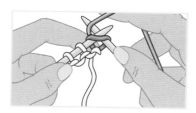

2 Take the yarn around and under the point of the right-hand needle.

3 Draw the new loop on the right-hand needle through the stitch on the left-hand needle.

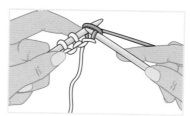

4 Slide the stitch off the left-hand needle. This has formed one knit stitch on the right-hand needle.

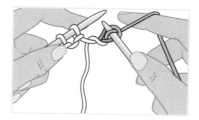

Repeat until all stitches on the left-hand needle have been transferred to the right-hand needle. This is the end of the row. Swap the right-hand needle into your left hand and begin the next row in exactly the same way.

# Purl Stitch

This is the reverse of the knit stitch. Each stitch is created with a four-step process. Hold the yarn at the front of the work – this is the side facing you.

1   Place the needle with the cast-on stitches in your left hand, insert the right-hand needle into the front of the first stitch on the left-hand needle from right to left.

Repeat these four steps to the end of the row.

2   Take the yarn over and around the point of the right-hand needle.

3   Draw the new loop on the right-hand needle through the stitch on the left-hand needle.

4   Slide the stitch off the left-hand needle. This has formed one purl stitch on the right-hand needle.

**Garter stitch**
Rows of knit stitch build up to form an interlocking fabric, which is called garter stitch (g st). It has ridges on the front and back and is identical from either side, so it is reversible. It forms a flat and fairly thick fabric that does not curl at the edges.

**Stockinette stitch**
Making alternate knit and purl rows creates stockinette (stocking) stitch. The knit rows are the right side of the fabric and the purl rows are the wrong side. Instructions for stockinette stitch in knitting patterns can be written as follows:
Row 1 RS Knit
Row 2 Purl
Or alternatively: Work in st st (1 row k, 1 row p), beg with a k row.

# Increasing & Decreasing

Many projects are not square or rectangular and therefore need to be shaped by adding or removing stitches. This is called increasing and decreasing.

## Increasing Stitches

### Make 1 (M1)

This method allows you to create a new stitch in between two existing stitches using the horizontal thread that lies between the stitches. Twisting the stitch prevents a hole appearing and makes your increase practically invisible.

**To twist M1 to the left**

1 Work to the position of the increase and insert the left-hand needle under the horizontal strand between the next two stitches from front to back.

**To twist M1 to the right**

1 Work to the position of the increase and insert the left-hand needle under the horizontal strand between the next two stitches from back to front.

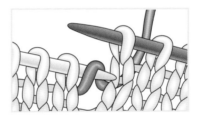

2 Knit this loop through the back to twist it.

2 Knit this loop through the back to twist it.

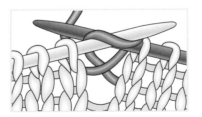

2 Knit this loop through the back to twist it.

# Knit into front and back (Kf&b)

This method is most often used at the edges of the knitted piece. If done neatly, it is virtually invisible within the pattern of stitches. Make sure you keep an even tension as you add the stitches; when you are knitting into the same stitch twice, it is easy to make it very tight and therefore very difficult to knit.

**On a knit row** Knit the first stitch on the left-hand needle in the usual way, but instead of sliding the stitch off the left-hand needle as you would normally do, still keeping the yarn at the back of the work, knit into the back of the same stitch. Then slide the stitch off the left-hand needle. You now have two stitches on the right-hand needle and have therefore created a stitch.

**On a purl row** Purl the first stitch on the left-hand needle in the usual way, but instead of sliding the stitch off the left-hand needle as you would normally do, still keeping the yarn at the front of the work, purl into the back of the same stitch. Then slide the stitch off the left-hand needle.

## Knit into front, back and front

This increases two stitches instead of one: simply knit into the front, back and then the front again of the same stitch.

## Multiple yarn overs (Yos)

These are used to make the holes on the Seed Stitch Set scarf edging.

**Yo 4 times** Wrap the yarn around the needle four times. On the return row, you must knit into the first loop of the yarn over, purl into the second, knit into the third and purl into the fourth loop.

**Yo 5 times** Wrap the yarn around the needle five times. On the return row, work into the first four loops of the yarn over as described for yo 4 times, and then knit into the fifth loop.

# Decreasing Stitches

Decreasing is used at the ends of rows or within the knitted fabric to reduce the number of stitches being worked on. Here are a number of ways to decrease one stitch.

## Knit two stitches together (K2tog)

This is the most straightforward method for decreasing and it does not change the appearance of the knitted fabric apart from making it narrower. Knit to where the decrease is to be made, insert the right-hand needle knitwise through the next two stitches on the left-hand needle. Knit these two stitches together as if they were one stitch.

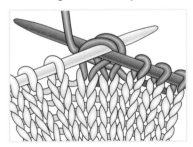

## Purl two stitches together (P2tog)

Purl to where the decrease is to be made, insert the right-hand needle purlwise through the next two stitches on the left-hand needle. Purl these two stitches together as if they were one stitch.

## Slip two stitches one at a time (Ssk) or (K2tog tbl)

1 Slip two stitches knitwise one at a time from left-hand needle to right-hand needle (they will be twisted).

2 Insert the left-hand needle from left to right through the fronts of these two stitches and knit together as one stitch.

## DECREASING TWO STITCHES AT ONCE

There are various ways of decreasing two stitches at once.

**K3tog** Work as k2tog, but knit three stitches together instead of two.

**P3tog** Work as p2tog, but purl three stitches together instead of two.

**K3tog tbl** Work as ssk (or k2tog tbl), but slip three stitches instead of two and knit them together.

## Sl2tog-k1-psso

**1** Insert the right-hand needle into the next two stitches as if to knit them together, and slip them off together on to the right-hand needle without knitting them. Knit the next stitch.

**2** With the tip of the left-hand needle, lift the two slipped stitches together over the knitted stitch and off the needle.

# Intarsia

Intarsia is the technique of colour knitting used to create coloured motifs or patterns. Each area of colour worked within the knitted piece is worked with a separate ball of yarn called a bobbin. As you work, the yarns are twisted where they meet so the blocks of colour are held together.

## Bobbins

When you knit with more than one colour of yarn, particularly for the intarsia method of colourwork, it helps to keep the yarns separate on bobbins to prevent them tangling and to make working easier. You can buy plastic bobbins and wrap a small amount of yarn on to each. Alternatively you can hand-wind your own small bobbins. Hand-winding a small bobbin is quick and easy.

### Hand-winding a bobbin
Leaving a long end, wind the yarn in a figure-of-eight around your thumb and little finger. Cut the yarn and use this cut end to tie a knot around the middle of the bobbin. Use the long end to pull the yarn from the middle of the bobbin. Use the long end to pull the yarn from the middle of the bobbin.

## TIP
If the knotted end becomes loose around the bobbin as you pull yarn out, keep tightening it otherwise the bobbin will unravel.

### Joining in a new colour

1 Insert the tip of the right-hand needle into the next stitch, place the cut end (4in/10cm from the end) of the new colour over the old colour and over the tip of the right-hand needle.

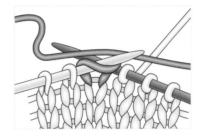

2 Take the working end of the new colour and knit the next stitch, pulling the cut end off the needle over the working end as the stitch is formed so it is not knitted in. Hold the cut end down against the back of the work.

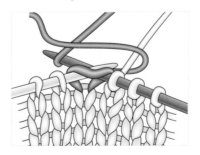

Once you've joined in all the colours that you need across the row, on the return row twist the yarns to join the blocks of colour together. When you change colour, always pick up the new colour from under the old yarn.

## Twisting yarns on a knit row
Insert the tip of the right-hand needle into the next stitch, pull the old colour to the left, pick up the new colour and bring it up behind the old colour. Knit the next stitch. The two yarns are twisted together.

## Twisting yarns on a purl row
Insert the tip of the right-hand needle into the next stitch, pull the old colour to the left, pick up the new colour and bring it up behind the old colour. Purl the next stitch. The two yarns are twisted together.

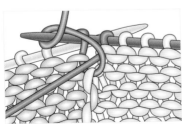

## Working from charts
Intarsia patterns are worked from charts. One square represents one stitch and a line of stitches represents one row. The rows are numbered: knit rows (RS rows) are odd numbers and are read from right to left; purl rows (WS rows) are even numbers and are read from left to right. Start knitting from the bottom right-hand corner of the chart at row 1.

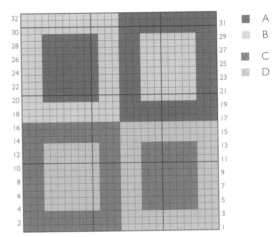

## Sewing in loose ends
Finish a piece of intarsia knitting by sewing in and cutting off any stray ends. Where the two colours are twisted together, you will see a line of loops. Using a large-eyed tapestry needle, darn in the end along this line in one direction and then back again for a few stitches. Block the piece and push any distorted stitches back into place with the end of a tapestry needle.

# Suppliers

Contact the manufacturers for your local stockist or go to their websites for stockist and mail order information.

## Colinette

www.colinette.com
**(USA) Paradise Fibers**
225 W Indiana,
Spokane, WA 99205
Tel: 001 888 320 7746
www.paradisefibers.com
**(UK) Colinette Yarns Ltd**
Banwy Workshops,
Llanfair Caereinion, SY21 0SG
Tel: 01938 810128
www.colinette.com
e-mail: feedback@colinette.com

## Debbie Bliss

www.debbieblissonline.com
**(USA) Knitting Fever Inc.**
315 Bayview Avenue,
Amityville, NY 11701
Tel: 516 546 3600
e-mail: admin@knittingfever.com
www.knittingfever.com
**(UK) Designer Yarns Ltd**
Units 8–10 Newbridge Industrial
Estate, Pitt Street, Keighley, West
Yorkshire, BD21 4PQ
Tel: 01535 664222
www.designeryarns.uk.com
e-mail: david@designeryarns.uk.com
**(AUS) Prestige Yarns Pty Ltd**
PO Box 39, Bulli, NSW 2516
Tel: 02 4285 6669
e-mail: info@prestigeyarns.com
www.prestigeyarns.com

## DMC

**(USA) The DMC Corporation**
10 Basin Drive, Suite 130,
Kearney, NJ 07032
Tel: 973 589 0606
www.dmc-usa.com
**(UK) DMC Creative World Ltd**
Unit 21 Warren Park Way,
Warrens Park, Enderby,
Leicester, LE18 4SA
Tel: 0116 275 4000
www.dmccreative.co.uk

**(AUS)** For a list of stockists go to their website at www.dmc.com

## GGH

www.ggh-garn.de
**(USA) My Muench Yarns Inc**
1323 Scott Street,
Petaluma, CA 94954-1135
Tel: 707 763 9477
e-mail: info@muenchyarns.com
www.muenchyarns.com
**(UK) Loop**
15 Camden Passage,
Islington, London, N1 8EA
Tel: 020 7288 1160
e-mail: loopknittingshop@yahoo.
co.uk
www.loopknittingshop.com

## Louisa Harding

www.louisaharding.co.uk
**(USA) Knitting Fever Inc.**
315 Bayview Avenue,
Amityville, NY 11701
Tel: 516 546 3600
e-mail: admin@knittingfever.com
www.knittingfever.com
**(UK) Designer Yarns Ltd**
Units 8–10 Newbridge Industrial
Estate, Pitt Street, Keighley, West
Yorkshire, BD21 4PQ
Tel: 01535 664222
www.designeryarns.uk.com
e-mail: david@designeryarns.
uk.com

## Noro

www. esiakunoro.com
**(USA) Knitting Fever Inc.**
315 Bayview Avenue,
Amityville, NY 11701
Tel: 516 546 3600
e-mail: admin@knittingfever.com
www.knittingfever.com
**(UK) Designer Yarns Ltd**
Units 8–10 Newbridge Industrial
Estate, Pitt Street, Keighley, West
Yorkshire, BD21 4PQ
Tel: 01535 664222
www.designeryarns.uk.com
e-mail: david@designeryarns.
uk.com
**(AUS) Prestige Yarns Pty Ltd**
PO Box 39, Bulli, NSW 2516
Tel: 02 4285 6669
e-mail: info@prestigeyarns.com
www.prestigeyarns.com

**Patons**

320 Livingstone Avenue South,
Box 40,
Listowel, ON, Canada, N4W 3H3
Tel: 888 368 8401
www.patonsyarns.com
**(UK) Coats Crafts UK**
Green Lane Mill, Holmfirth,
West Yorkshire, HD9 2DX
Tel: 01325 394237
e-mail: consumer.ccuk@coats.com
www.coatscrafts.co.uk

**The Rare Yarns Company**

155 Hardy Street, Nelson 7011,
New Zealand
Tel: 3 548 4016
e-mail: info@rareyarns.co.nz
www.rareyarns.co.nz

**Rowan**

www.knitrowan.com
**(USA) Westminster Fibers Inc**
165 Ledge Street, Nashua,
New Hampshire 03060
Tel: 800 445 9276
www.westminsterfibers.com
e-mail: info@westminsterfibers.
com
**(UK) Rowan**
Green Lane Mill, Holmfirth,
West Yorkshire, HD9 2DX
Tel: 01484 681881
e-mail: mail@knitrowan.com
**(AUS) Australian Country
Spinners Pty Ltd**
Level 7, 409 St. Kilda Road,
Melbourne, Victoria 3004
Tel: 03 9380 3888
email: tkohut@auspinners.com.au

**Rowan Classic Yarns (RCY)**

www.ryclassic.com
**(USA) Westminster Fibers Inc**
165 Ledge Street, Nashua,
New Hampshire 03060
Tel: 800 445 9276
www.westminsterfibers.com
e-mail: info@westminsterfibers.
com
**(UK) RYC**
Green Lane Mill, Holmfirth,
West Yorkshire, HD9 2BR
Tel: 01484 681881
e-mail: mail@ryclassic.com
**(AUS) Australian Country
Spinners Pty Ltd**
Level 7, 409 St. Kilda Road,
Melbourne,
Victoria 3004
Tel: (03) 9380 3888
email: tkohut@auspinners.com.au

**Sirdar**

www.sirdar.co.uk
**(USA) Knitting Fever Inc.**
315 Bayview Avenue,
Amityville, NY 11701
Tel: 516 546 3600
e-mail: admin@knittingfever.com
www.knittingfever.com
**(UK) Sirdar Spinning Ltd**
Flanshaw Lane, Wakefield,
West Yorkshire, WF2 9ND
Tel: 01924 371501
e-mail: enquiries@sirdar.co.uk
**(AUS) Creative Images**
PO Box 106, Hastings, Victoria
3915
Tel: 03 5979 1555
e-mail: creative@peninsula.
starway.net.au

**Twilleys**

www.tbramsden.co.uk
**(UK) Twilleys of Stamford**
Netherfield Road, Guiseley,
Leeds, LS20 9PD
Tel: 01943 872264
e-mail: twilleys@tbramsden.co.uk

A DAVID & CHARLES BOOK
© F&W Media International, LTD 2013

David & Charles is an imprint of F&W Media
International, Ltd
Brunel House, Forde Close, Newton Abbot,
TQ12 4PU, UK

F&W Media International, Ltd is a subsidiary of
F+W Media, Inc
10151 Carver Road, Cincinnati OH45242, USA

First published in the UK and US in 2013
Published in the US as *Stitch Craft Create Quick Knits*

Content, layout and photography © F&W Media
International, LTD 2013

Names of manufacturers and product ranges are
provided for the information of readers, with no
intention to infringe copyright or trademarks.
A catalogue record for this book is available from the
British Library.

ISBN-13: 978-1-4463-0389-4 paperback (UK)
ISBN-10: 1-4463-0389-6 paperback (UK)

ISBN-13: 978-1-4463-0395-5 paperback (US)
ISBN-10: 1-4463-0395-0 paperback (US)

Printed in China by RR Donnelley
for F&W Media International, LTD
Brunel House, Forde Close, Newton Abbot,
TQ12 4PU, UK

10 9 8 7 6 5 4 3 2 1

Publisher: Alison Myer
Multi-Channel Content Editor: James Brooks
Art Editor: Charly Bailey
Project Photographer: Sian Irvine
Production Manager: Bev Richardson

F+W Media, Inc. publishes high-quality books on a wide
range of subjects. For more great book ideas visit:
**www.stitchcraftcreate.co.uk**